Alfred's Premier Piano C...

Universal Edition

Dennis Alexander • Gayle Kowalchyk • E. L. Lancaster • Victoria McArthur • Martha Mier

Level 1B builds upon the strong foundation begun in Level 1A.

- Note-reading skills continue to be developed by recognizing landmark notes (not hand positions) and reading by intervals from these notes.
- Rhythm patterns from Level 1A are reviewed and new patterns are added.
- Technical *Workouts* focus on a gradual development of the skills necessary for playing hands together.

Lesson Book 1B is designed to correlate with Theory and Performance Books 1B of *Alfred's Premier Piano Course*. When used together, they offer a fully integrated and unparalleled comprehensive approach to piano instruction.

To provide a performance model and a practice companion, a compact disc recording is included with the book. Each title is performed twice on acoustic piano—a *performance* tempo and a slower *practice* tempo.

See page 49 for information on the CD. Flash Cards 1B (22366) and a General MIDI Disk 1B (23259) are available separately.

Edited by Morton Manus

Cover Design by Ted Engelbart
Interior Design by Tom Gerou
Illustrations by Jimmy Holder
Music Engraving by Linda Lusk

Copyright © MMV by Alfred Publishing Co., Inc.
All Rights Reserved. Printed in USA.

Contents

Premier Music Review	2
Tie	8
New Note A (Treble)	11
Legato (Slur)	14
Staccato	15
Intervals – Interval of a 2nd	18
Interval of a 3rd	19
New Landmark Note—Treble C	22
Ritardando	23
New Notes B and D (Treble)	24
Moving Up from Treble G	25
New Landmark Note—Low G	26
New Notes A and B (Bass)	27
Phrase	27
Moving Up from Low G	28
8va	29
Interval of a 4th	30
Interval of a 5th	32
Fermata	33
Moving Up a Semitone—Sharp Sign	34
Incomplete Bar	37
Moving Down a Semitone—Flat Sign	42

Premier Music Review

Use with Alfred's Premier Theory Book Level 1B: pages 2–3.

1. **Matching Game:** Draw a line from the symbol to its matching name.

   f • crotchet

   p • forte—play loudly

   o • semibreve

   ♩ • minim

   ♩. • semibreve rest

   mf • minim rest

   ▬ • crotchet rest

   ♪ (half note) • dotted minim

   ▬ • piano—play softly

   𝄽 • mezzo forte—play moderately loud

2. **Time Signature:** What do the numbers mean? Fill in the blanks.

   4/4 Each bar gets _____ counts.
   Each _____ gets one beat.
   (draw the note)

   3/4 Each bar gets _____ counts.
   Each _____ gets one beat.
   (draw the note)

3. **Music Alphabet:** On the keyboard, write the name of each white key, beginning with the lowest A and ending with the highest G.

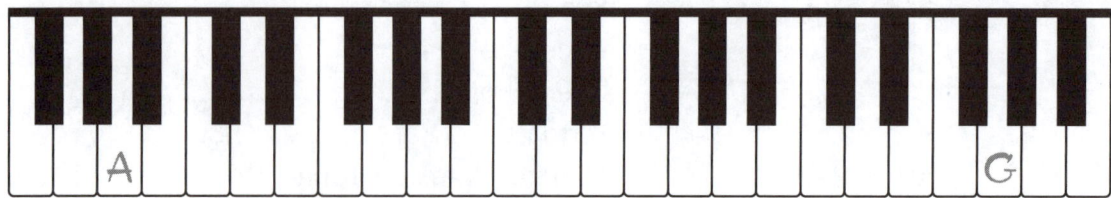

4. Write the counts (by bar) under the notes and rest. Then tap and count aloud.

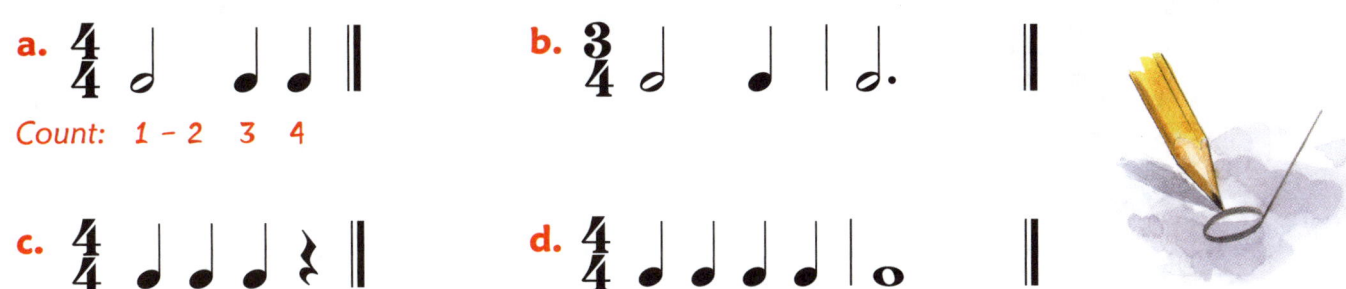

Count: 1 – 2   3   4

5. Name the Landmark Notes.   Then name the notes below.

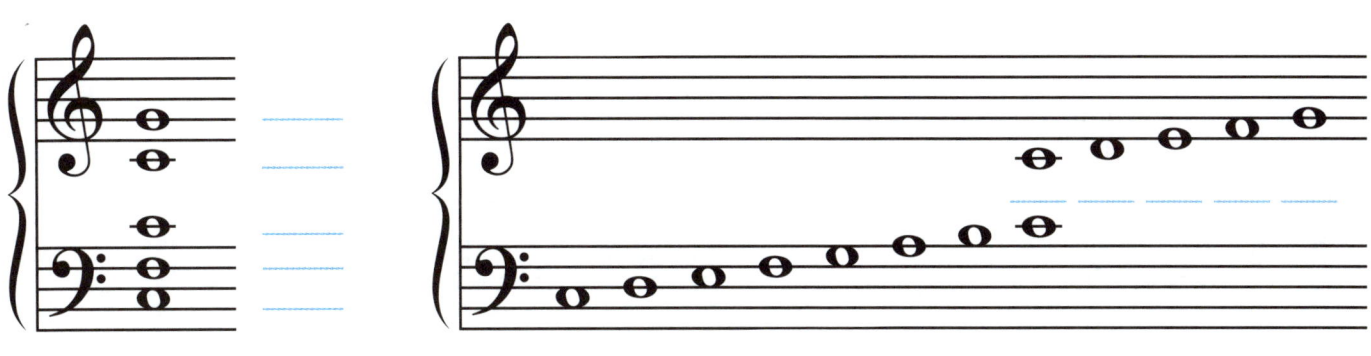

6. Name the notes in each bar. Then circle *up* or *down*; *step* or *skip*.

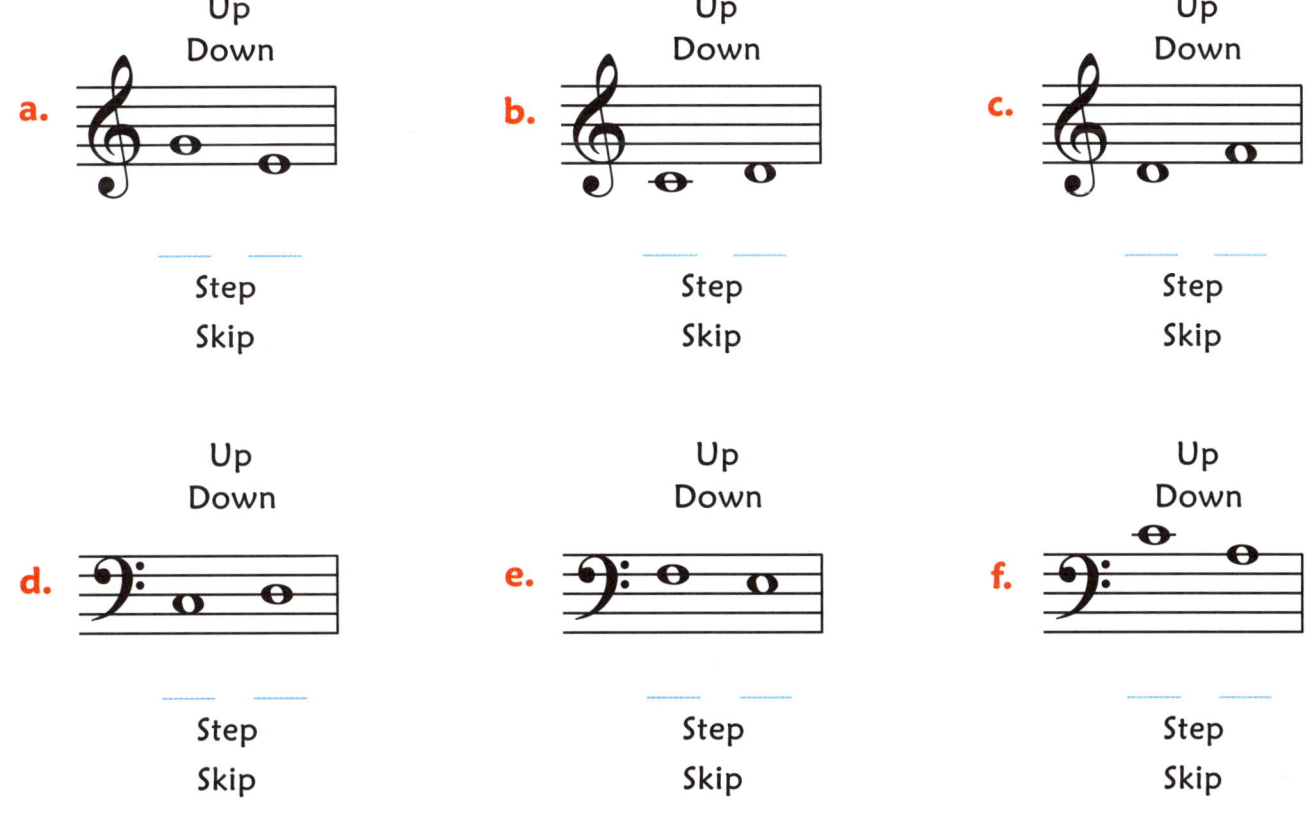

Theory Book: pages 4–5

Rhythm Review

Count: 1 2 3 1 - 2 - 3

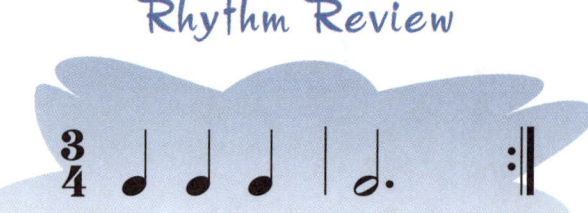

Tap and count the rhythm.

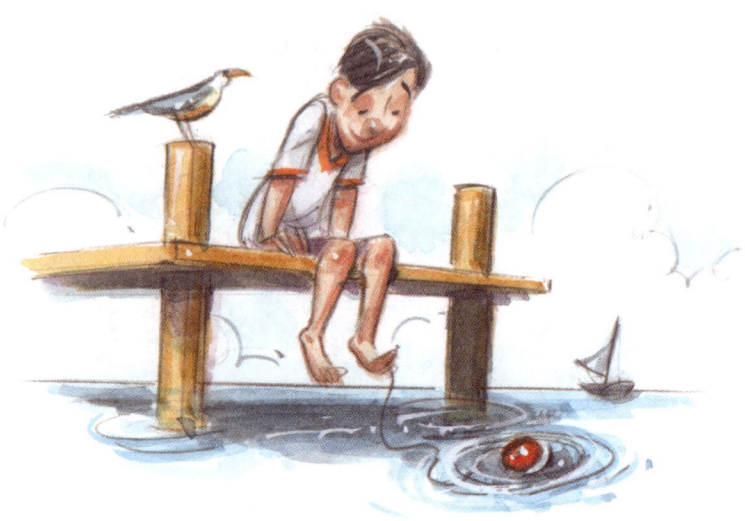

The Boat Dock

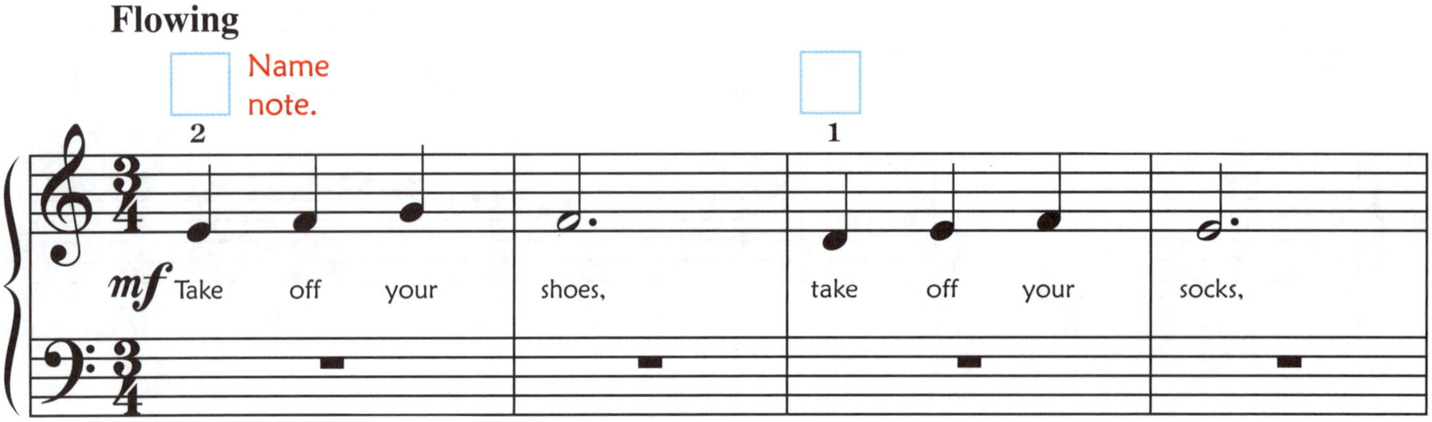
Flowing
Name note.
mf
Take off your shoes, take off your socks,

Duet: Student plays one octave higher.

Flowing
RH
CD 1/2
GM 1
LH
mp
5
9
pp
13
mp

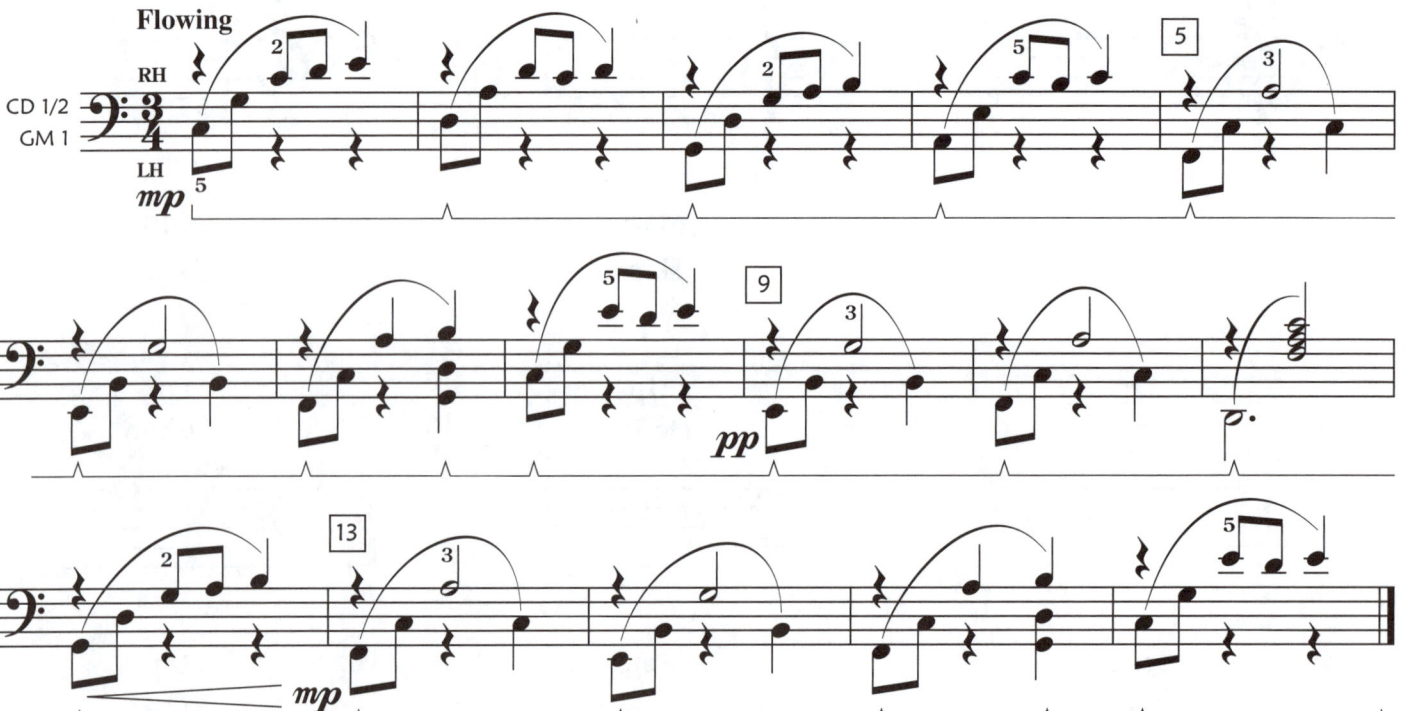

Practice Journal for Level 1B

For each piece:
- ✔ Check the time signature. Then tap the rhythm and count aloud by bar.
- ✔ Check the starting finger numbers for each hand and look for places where the hands move.
- ✔ Check the starting dynamic sign and look for places where dynamics change.
- ✔ Play and sing (or say) the note names.
- ✔ Play and count aloud.
- ✔ Play and sing (or say) the words (if any).

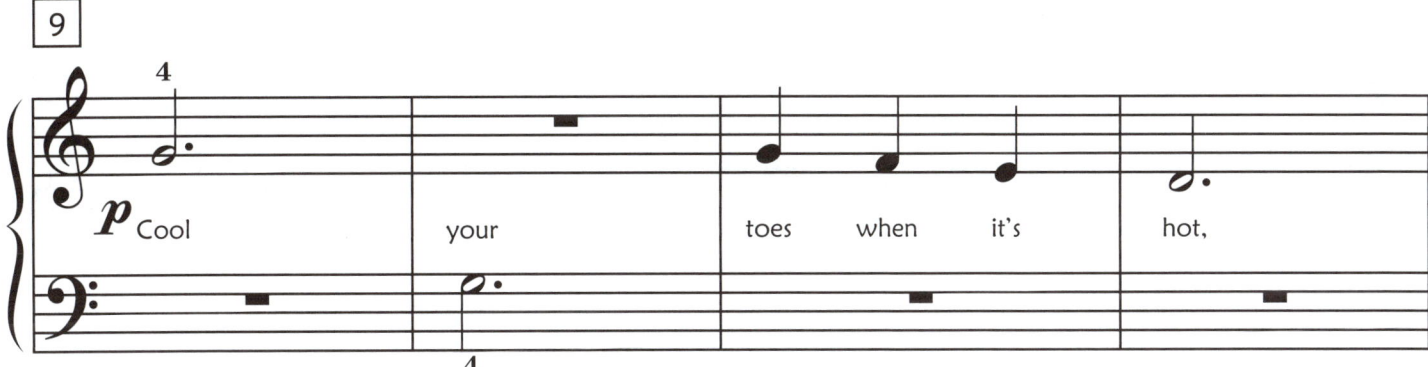

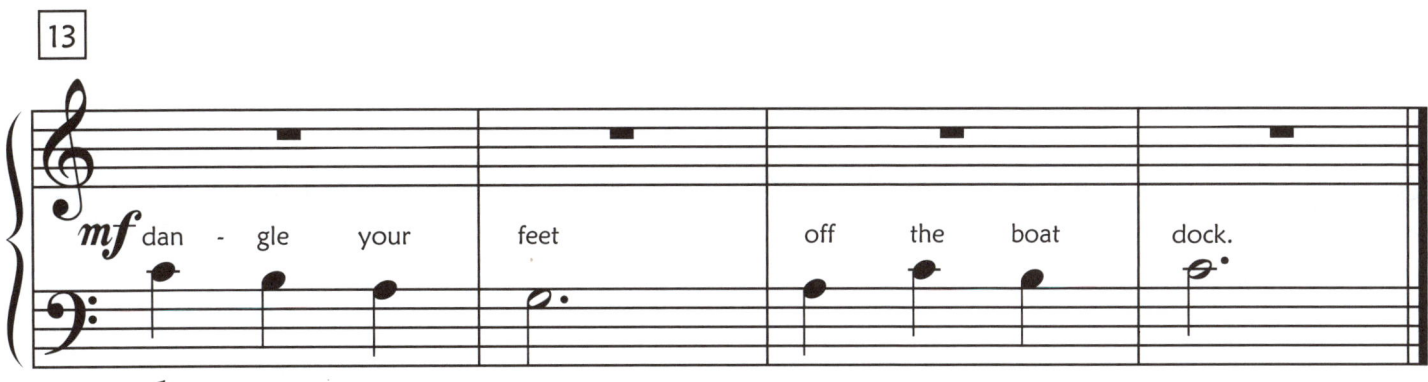

Closer Look — Circle the skips in the LH of *The Boat Dock*. How many are there? _____

Count: 1 2 3 4 1 2 3-4

Tap and count the rhythm.

At the Park

Imagination Station
Play At the Park *again*, changing at least 2 dynamic signs to those of your choice.

Duet: Student plays one octave higher.

Walk to School

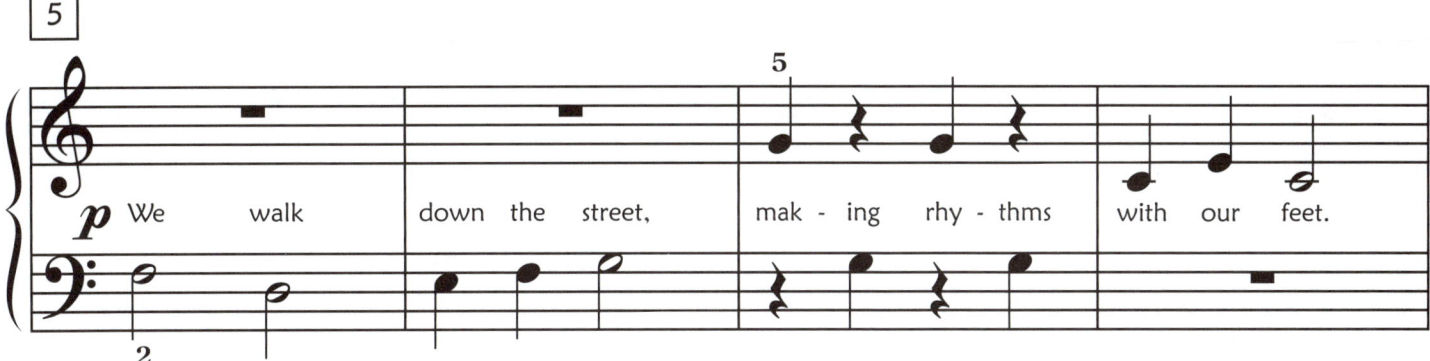

Duet: Student plays one octave higher.

Tie

A curved line that connects notes on the same line or space is called a **tie.** Play the first note and hold for the length of the combined notes.

Snorkelling

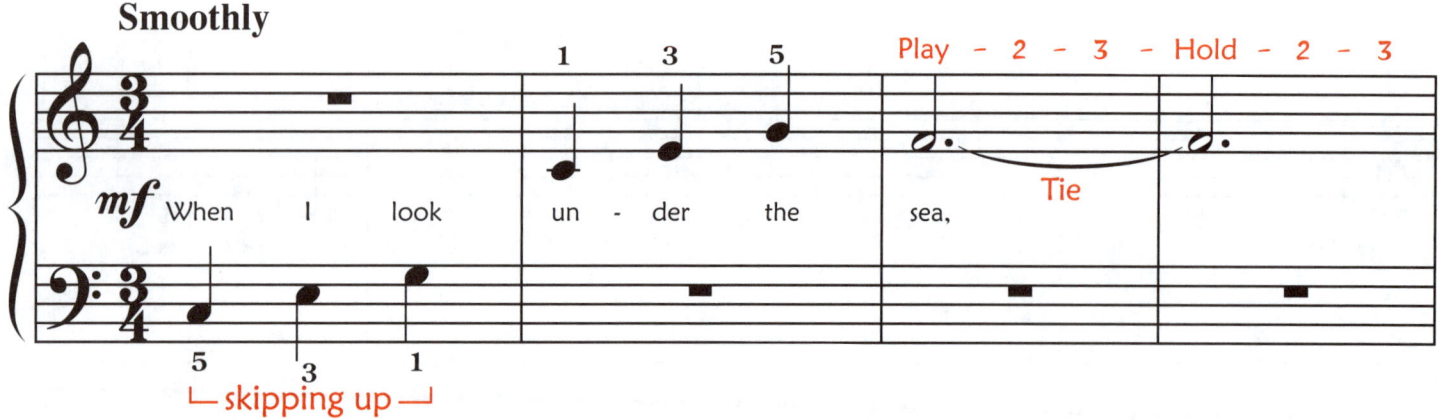

Duet: Student plays one octave higher.

Workout 1 Hands Together

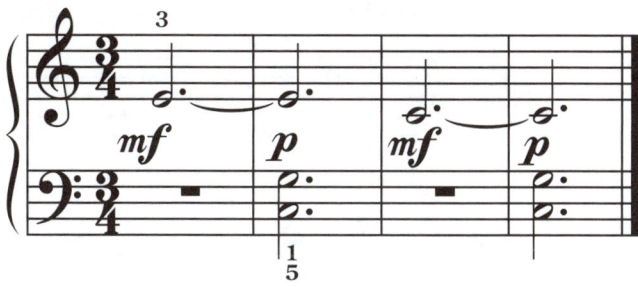

Play 3 times each day.

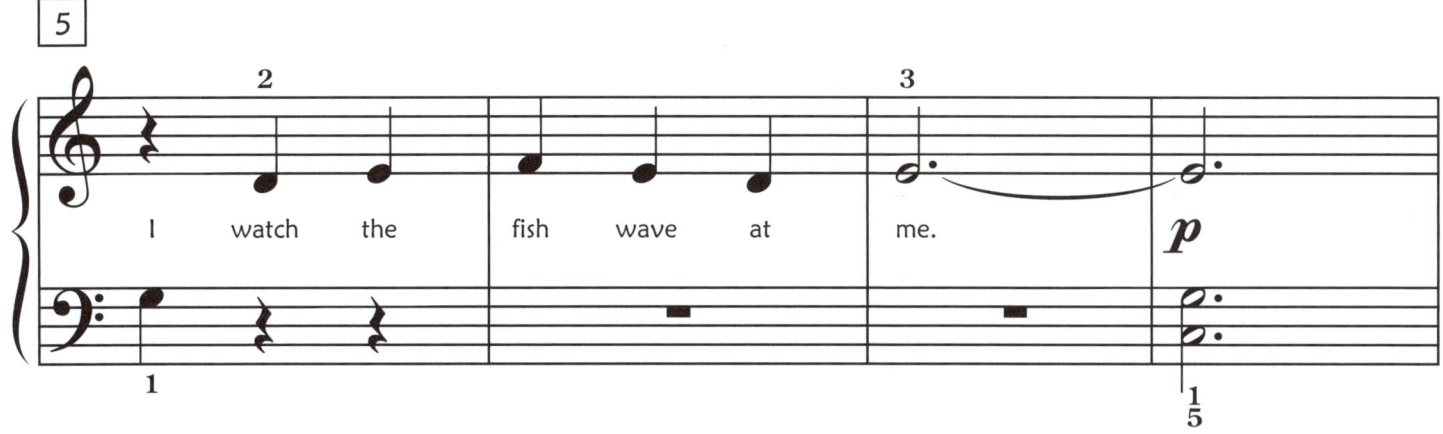

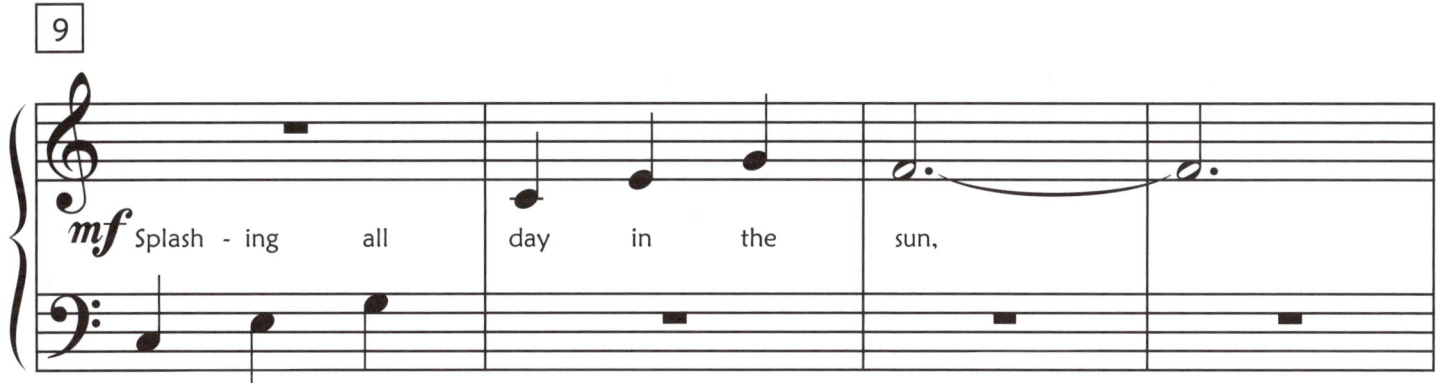

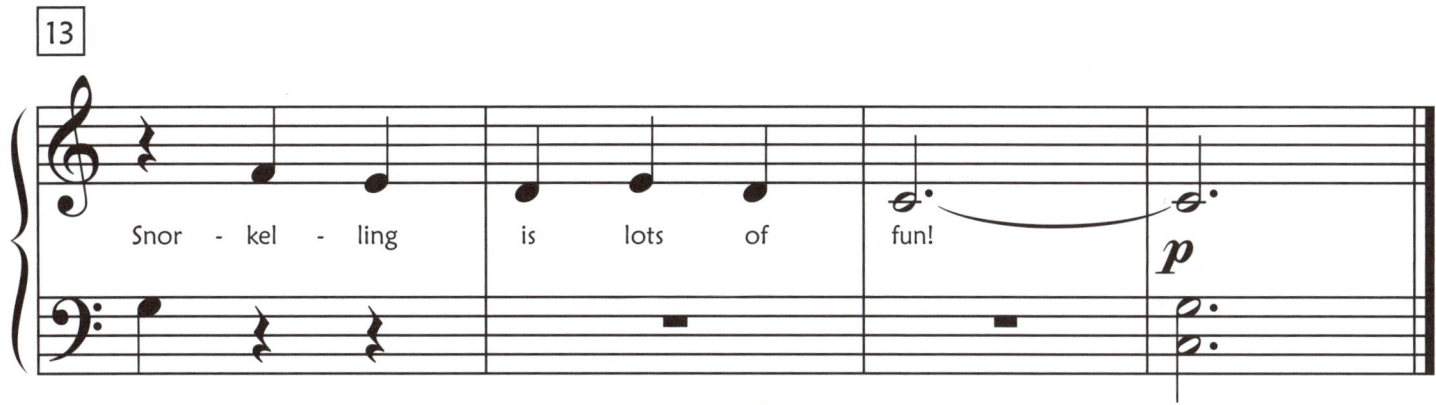

Closer Look *Circle the ties in Snorkelling.*

Opening Day

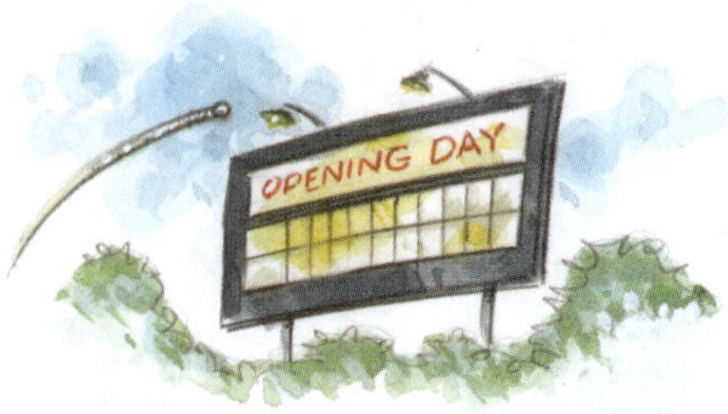

Count: 1 2 3 4 - 1-2-3-4

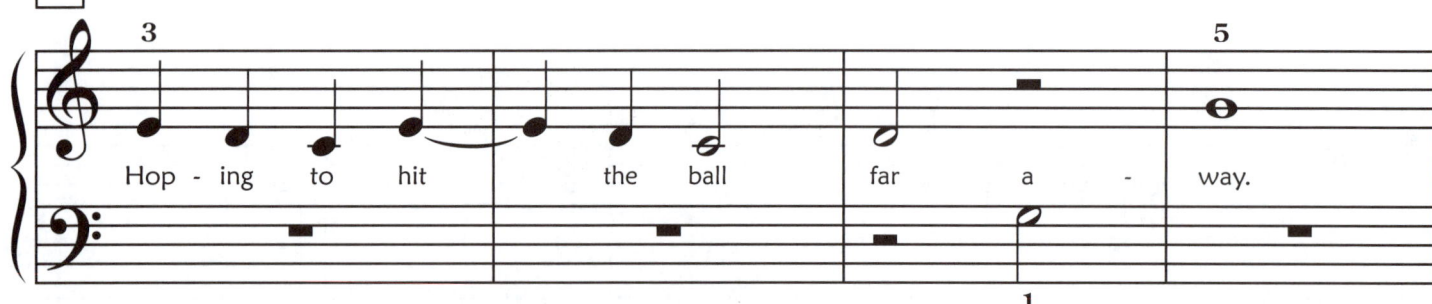

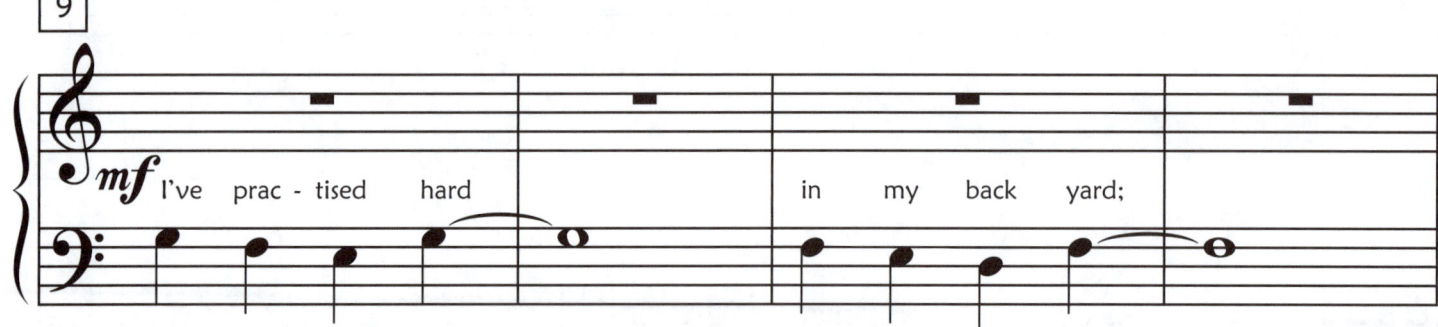

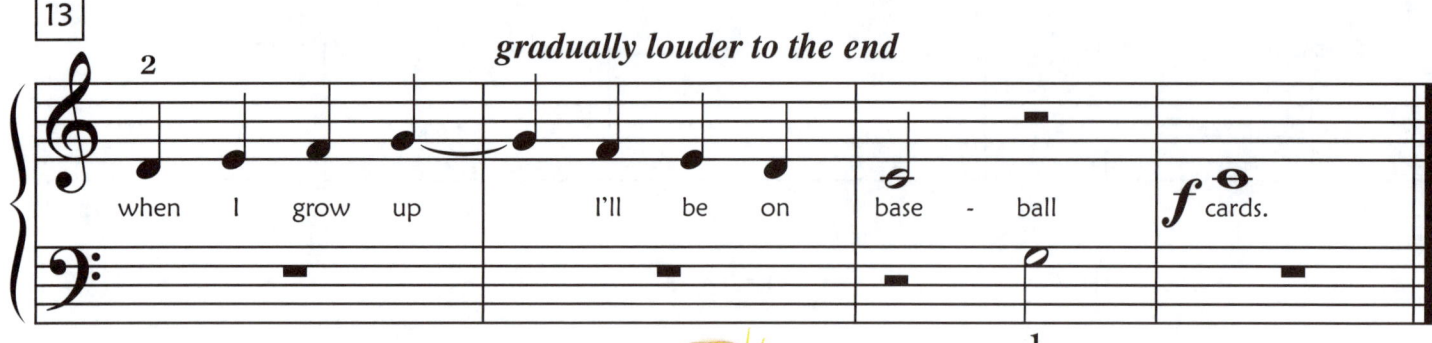

Closer Look — Circle 6 ties in Opening Day.

Duet: Student plays one octave higher.

New Note A

Step up from Treble G.

Workout 2 Hands Together

Play 3 times each day.

Green Tea

Relaxed

☐ Name note.

Water in the pot, heat it till it's ver-y hot. Put some green tea in, watch the leaves be-gin to spin. Green tea in my cup— drink it up!

Duet: Student plays one octave higher.

The Library

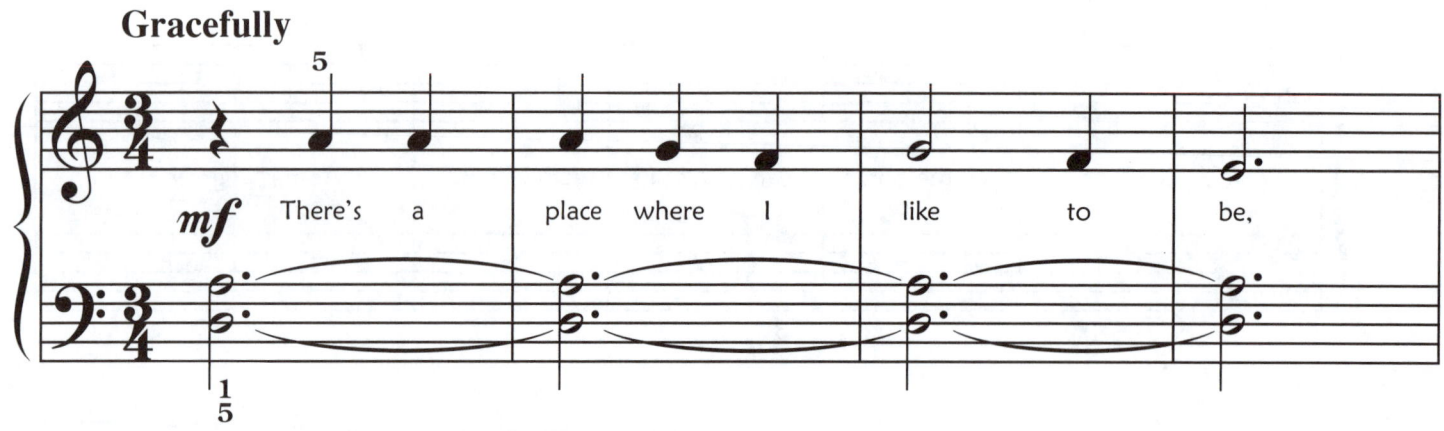

Duet: Student plays one octave higher.

Workout 3 Hands Together

Play 3 times each day.

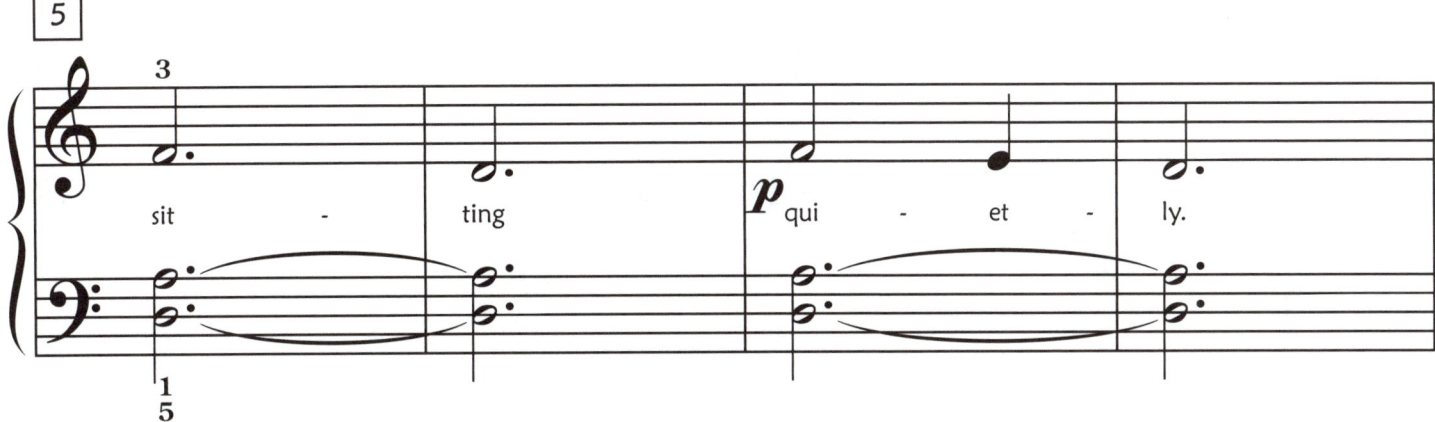

sit - ting qui - et - ly.

There are books you can bor - row for free

at the li - brar - y.

Premier Performer — *While playing The Library, count aloud "1-2-3" without pausing at the bar lines.*

Theory Book: page 14
Performance Book: page 6

Legato

Legato means to play the notes smoothly and connected.

A *slur* over or under the notes means to play *legato*.

Slur
Slur

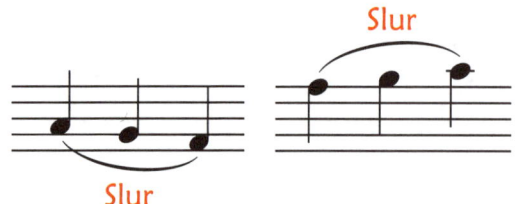

Workout 4 Smooth Connection

Count aloud as you play 3 times each day.

Press *down* one finger on the first count of each bar. Hold down each note.

a.
Ties
mf
1
2
3

b.
1
2
3
mf
Ties

Lift one finger *up* exactly as you press the next one down:

c.
Slur
mf
1

d.
1
mf
Slur

e.
mf
1

f.
1
mf

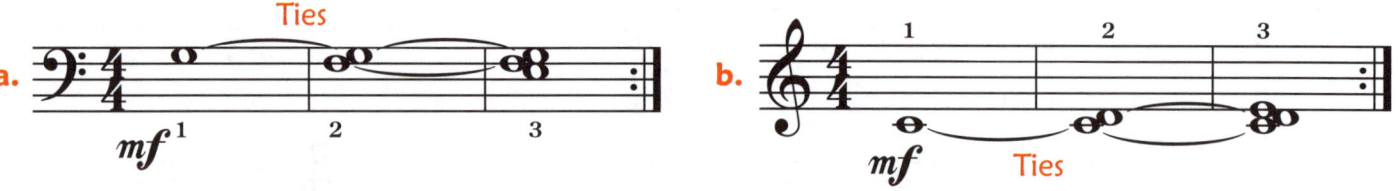

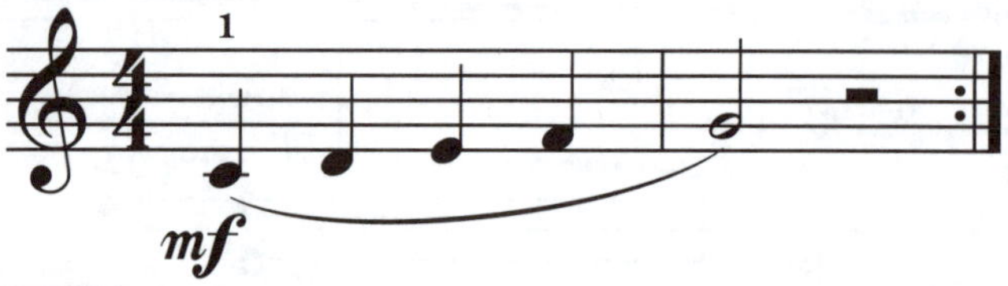

Smoothies

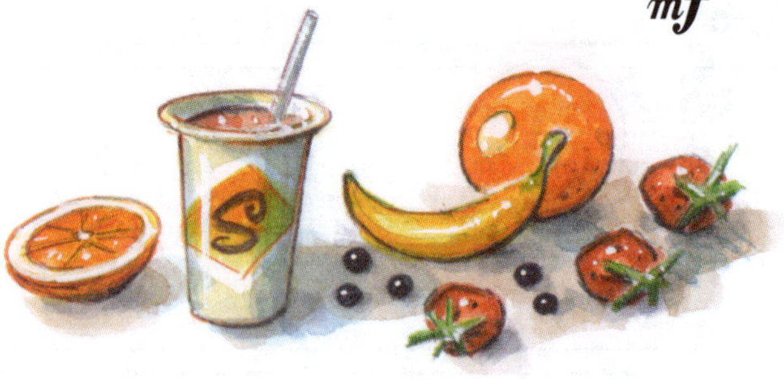

CD 15/16 GM 8

Smoothly
1
mf
In the blend - er we can make smooth-ies that taste just like shakes.
Milk and ice will go in first, blend with fruit, then quench your thirst.
1

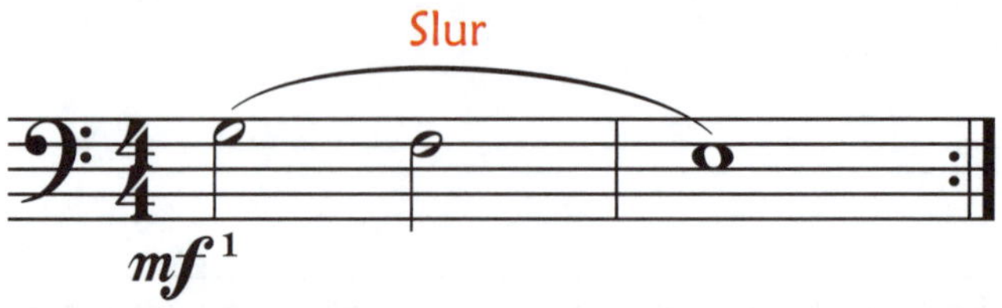

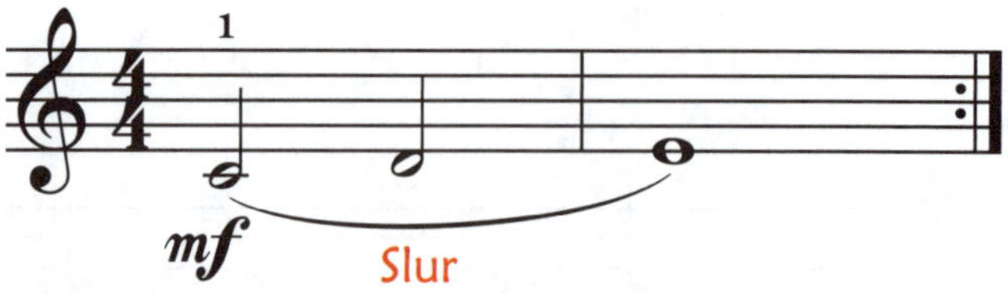

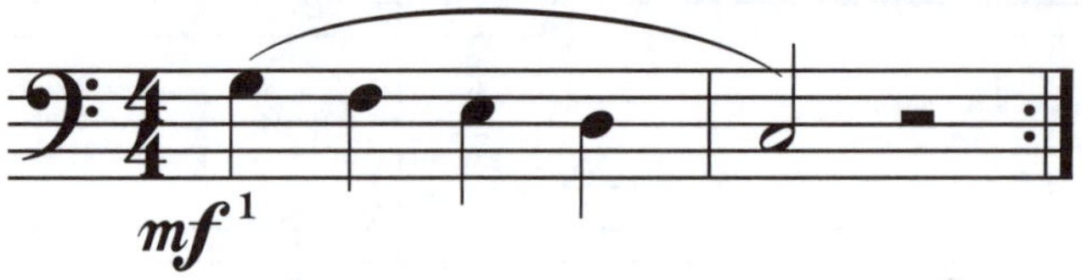

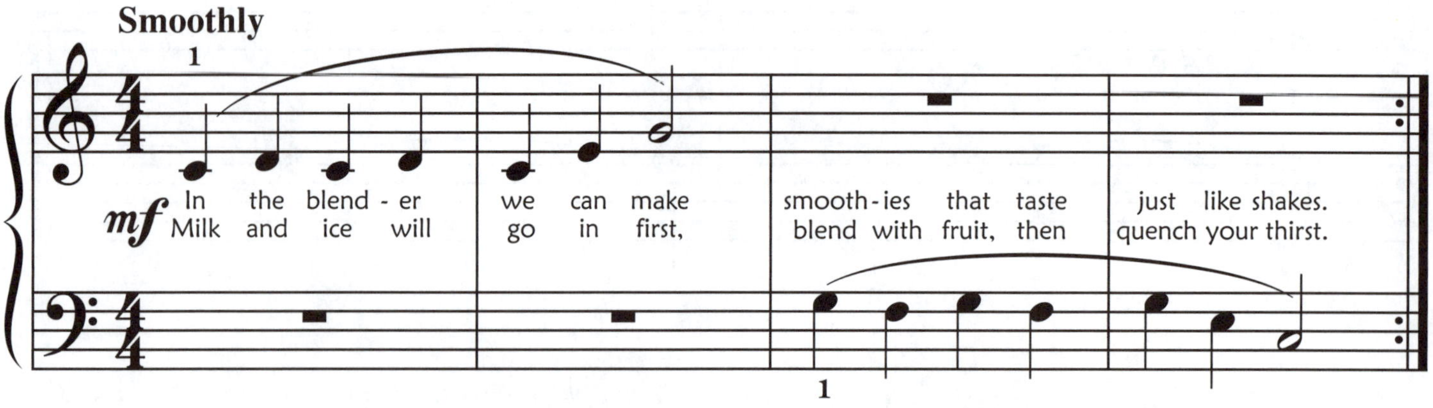

Theory Book: page 15
Performance Book: page 7

Staccato

Staccato means to play the notes short and detached.

A *dot* over or under a note means to play *staccato.*

Staccato
Staccato

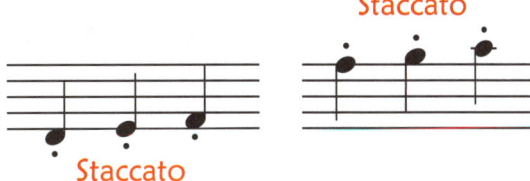

Workout 5 Tapping on My Door

- Make a loose fist with your LH. Lightly tap the closed keyboard cover with your knuckles, using a relaxed wrist to raise and lower your fist.
- Then uncurl your fingers into a rounded hand position. Using finger 3, tap 7 times on the keyboard cover with the same tapping motion.
- Repeat with RH.
- Using the same technique, play the following exercises. The 3rd finger moves quickly off the keys.

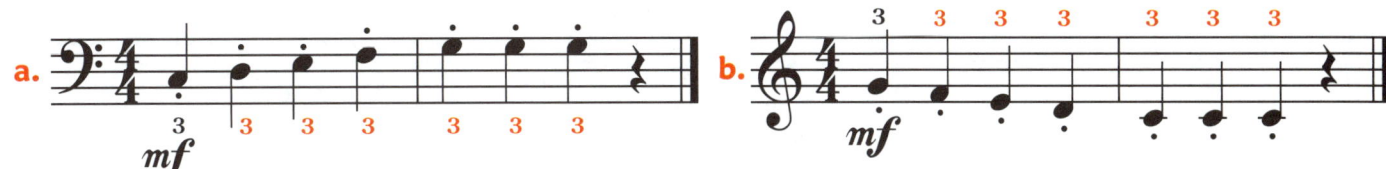

a.
b.
mf
mf

Crispy Chips

CHIPS

CD 17/18 GM 9

Crisply
mf
Here is some-thing good to eat, some-thing crunch-y, but not sweet.
5
Grab a bag of crisp - y chips, take a bite, then lick your lips.

Closer Look *Clap and count this rhythm:* ♩ ♩ ♩ 𝄽
Circle this rhythm pattern 4 times in Crispy Chips*.*

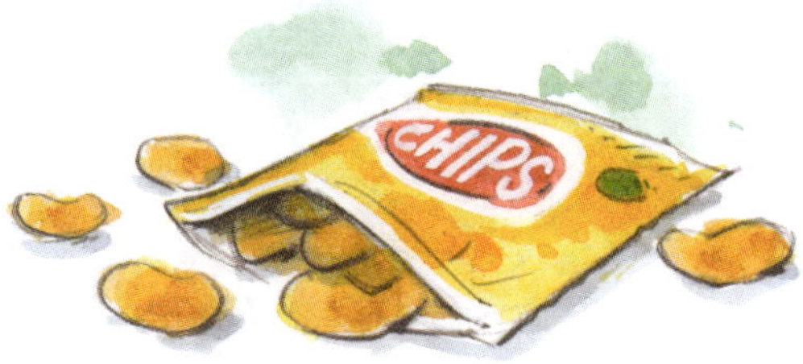

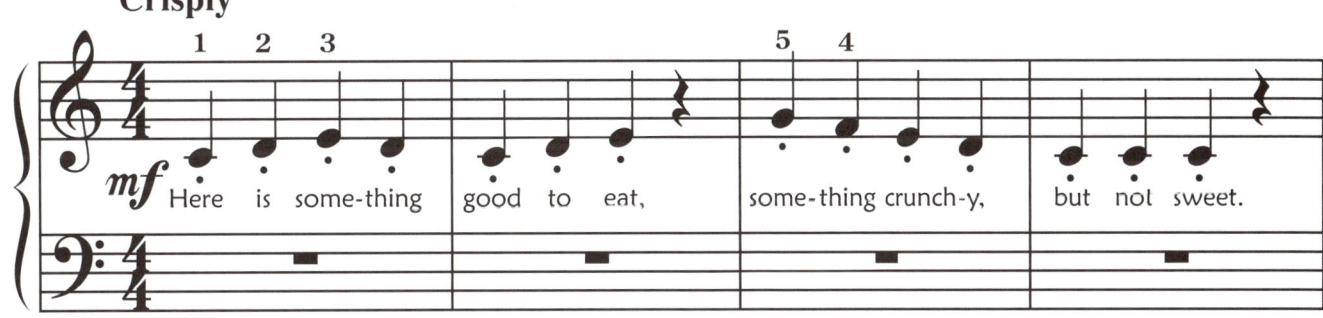

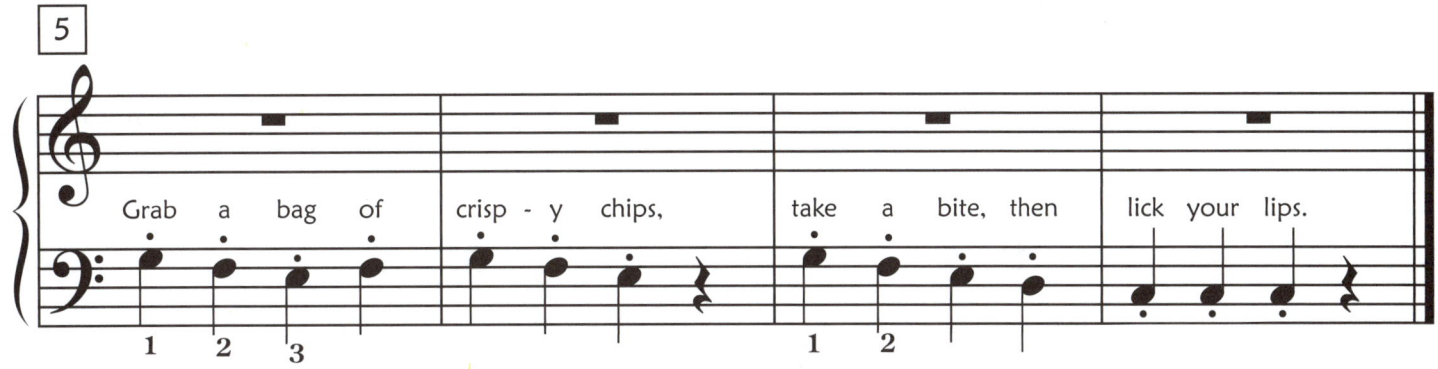

In the Pool
CD 19/20   GM 10

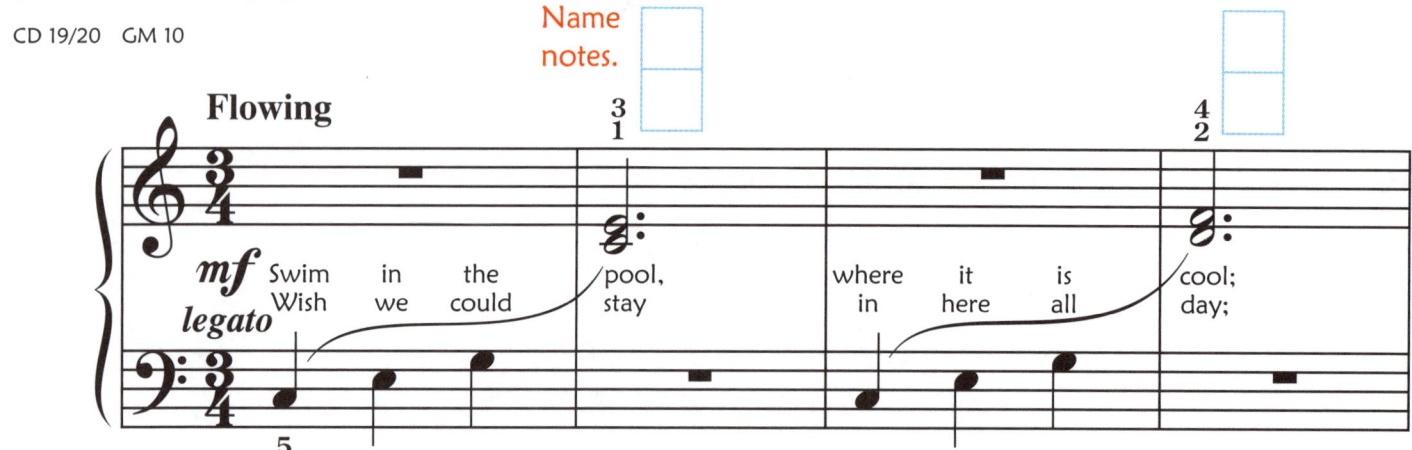

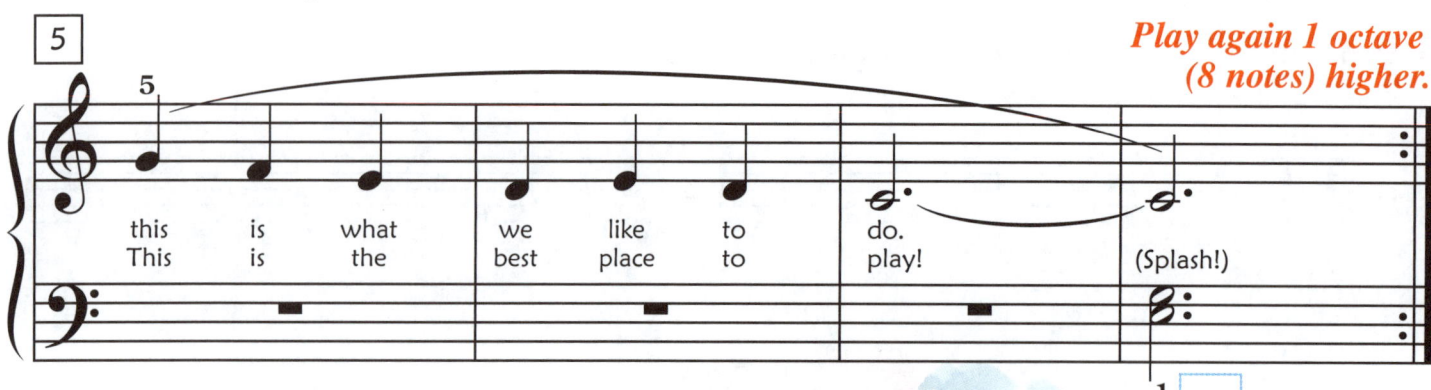

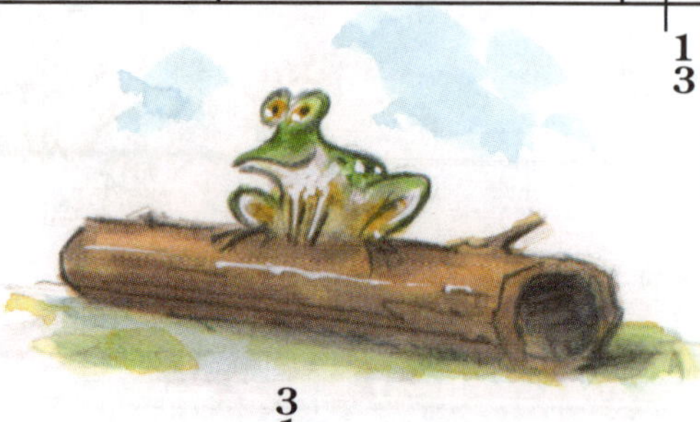

Catch That Frog!
CD 21/22   GM 11

My Pony

Count: 1 2 3 4   1 2 3 – 4

Tap and count aloud 3 times each day.

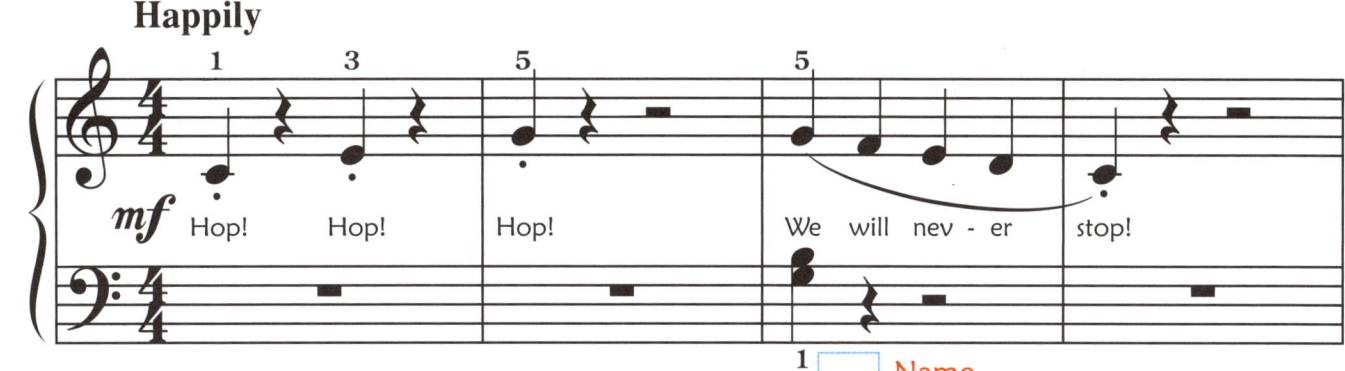

Name notes.

Move LH down

Premier Performer — Play line 2 of *My Pony* as legato as possible.

Duet: Student plays one octave higher.

Theory Book: page 18

Intervals

An *interval* is the distance from one note to another on the stave or keyboard, either *up* or *down*. Intervals are numbered: 2nd, 3rd, 4th, 5th, etc.

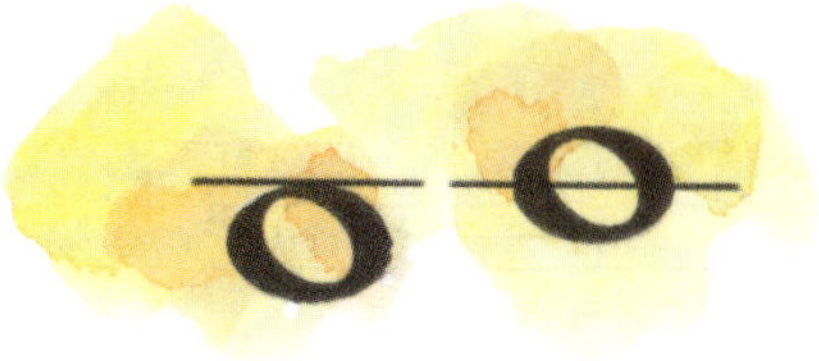

Interval of a 2nd

A **2nd** is the same as a *step*.

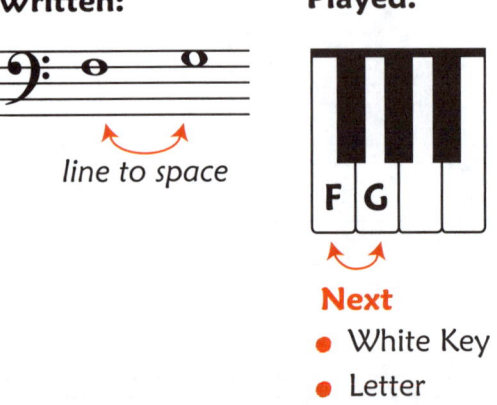

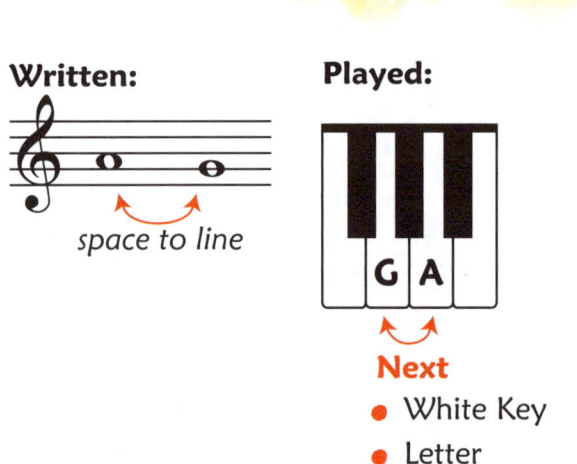

Written:

line to space

Played:

Next

- White Key
- Letter

Written:

space to line

Played:

Next

- White Key
- Letter

Melodic Interval

Notes played separately make a *melody*. An interval between two notes played *separately* is called a **melodic interval.**

melodic 2nd

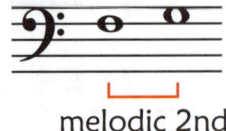

Harmonic Interval

Notes played together make *harmony*. An interval between two notes played *together* is called a **harmonic interval.**

harmonic 2nd

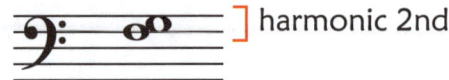

Listen as you play melodic and harmonic 2nds:

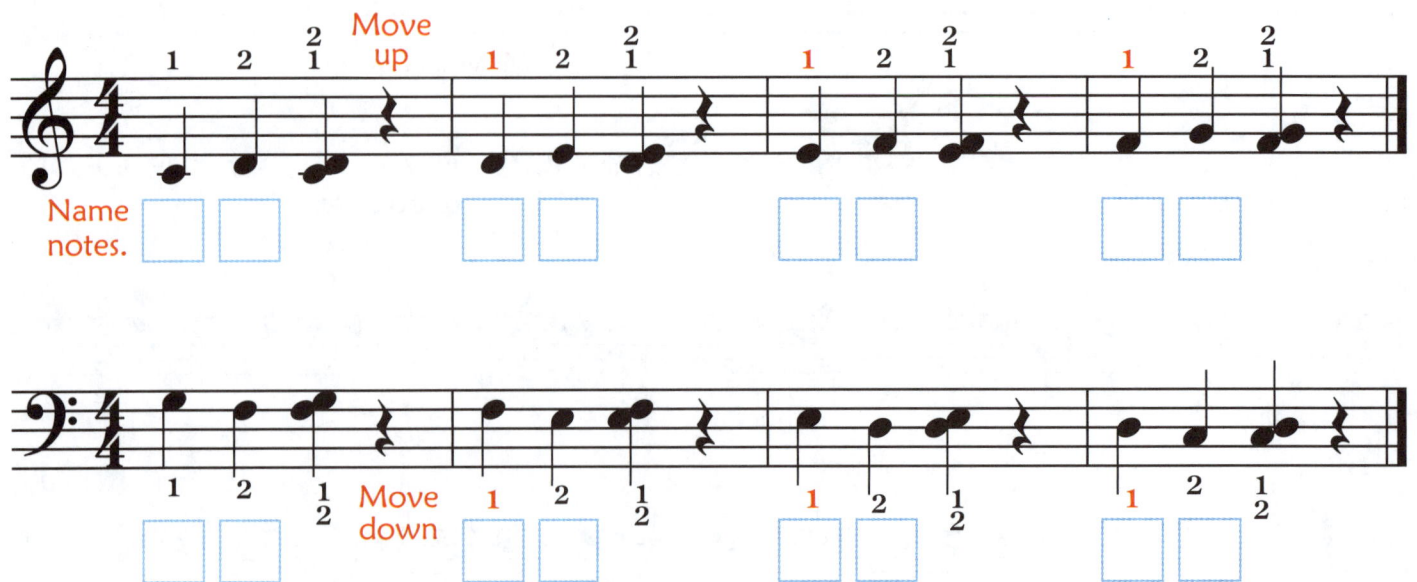

Theory Book: page 19
Performance Book: pages 8–9

Interval of a 3rd

A **3rd** is the same as a *skip*.

Written:

Played:

Skip 1
- White Key
- Letter

Written:

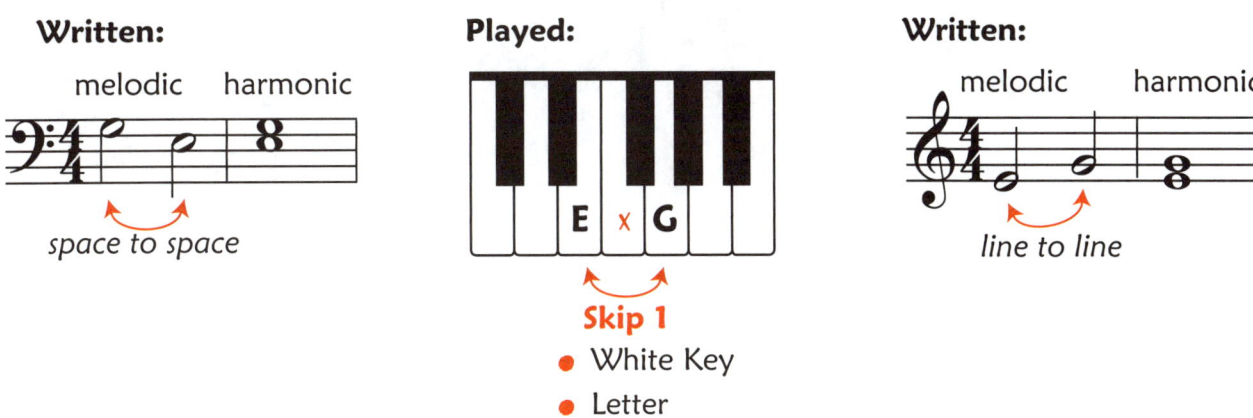

Listen as you play melodic and harmonic 3rds:

Name notes.

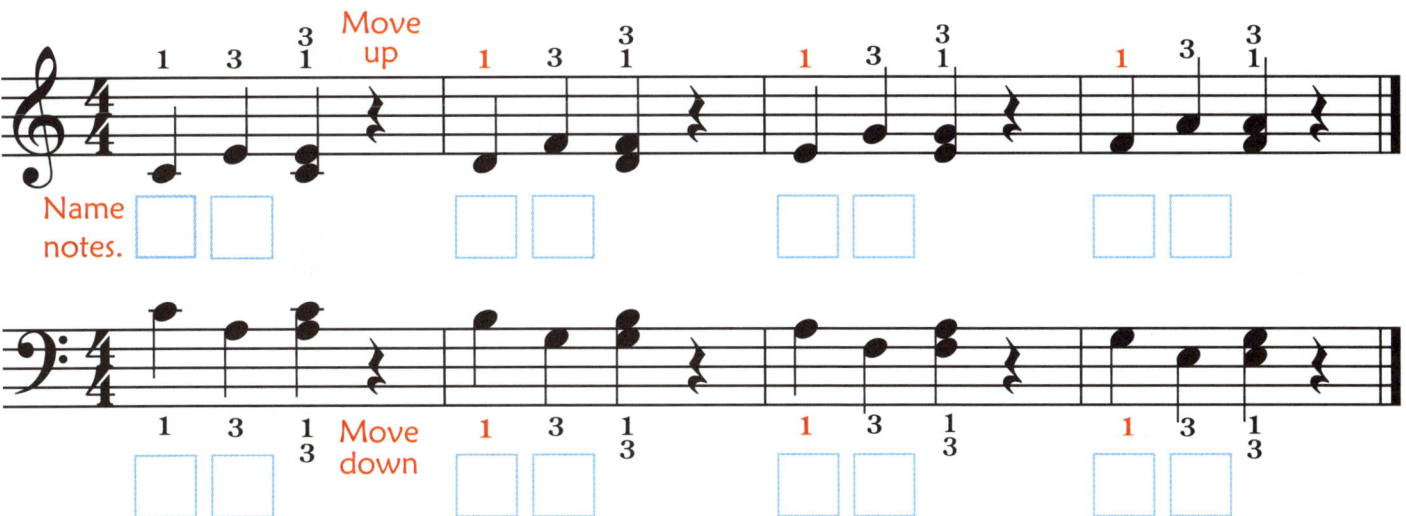

Finding 2nds and 3rds

a. Play then play the note that is *up* a 2nd. Name the note. ____

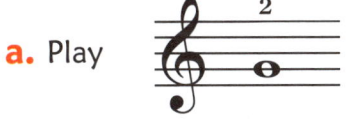

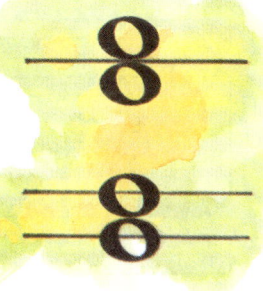

b. Play then play the note that is *down* a 3rd. Name the note. ____

c. Play then play the note that is *down* a 3rd. Name the note. ____

d. Play then play the note that is *up* a 2nd. Name the note. ____

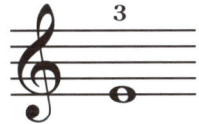

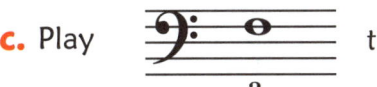

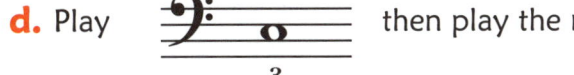

Popcorn

CD 25/26   GM 13

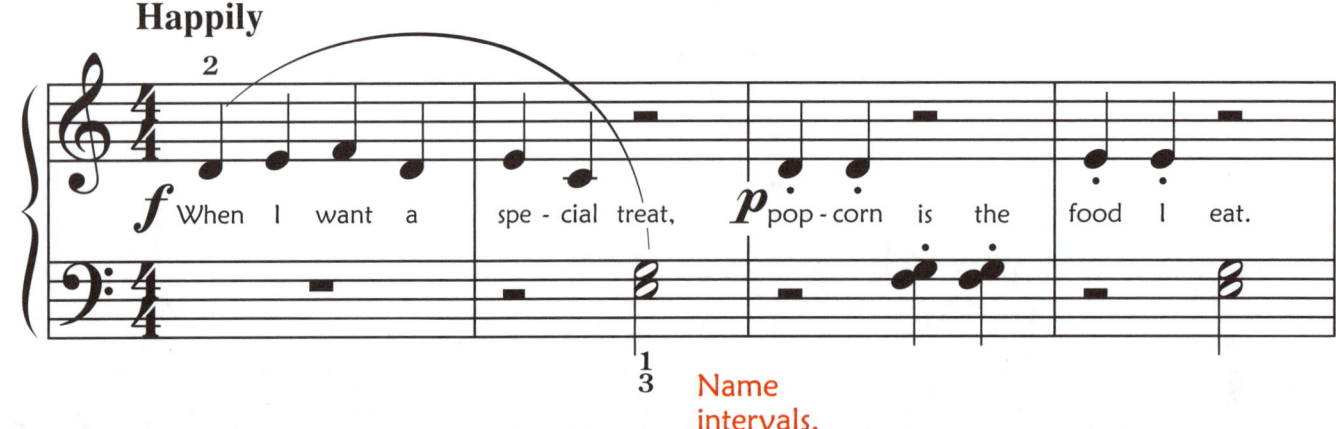

Name intervals.

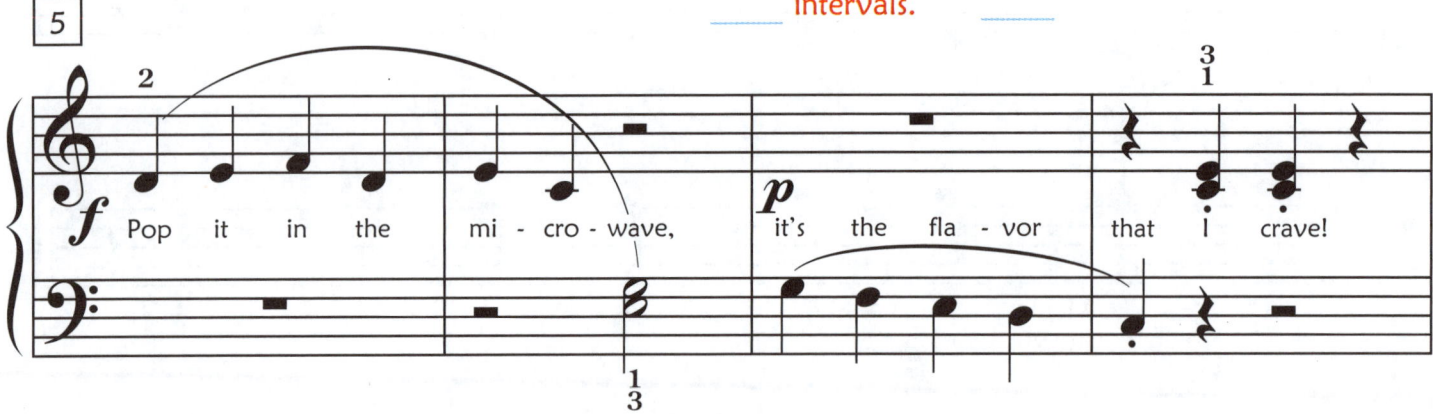

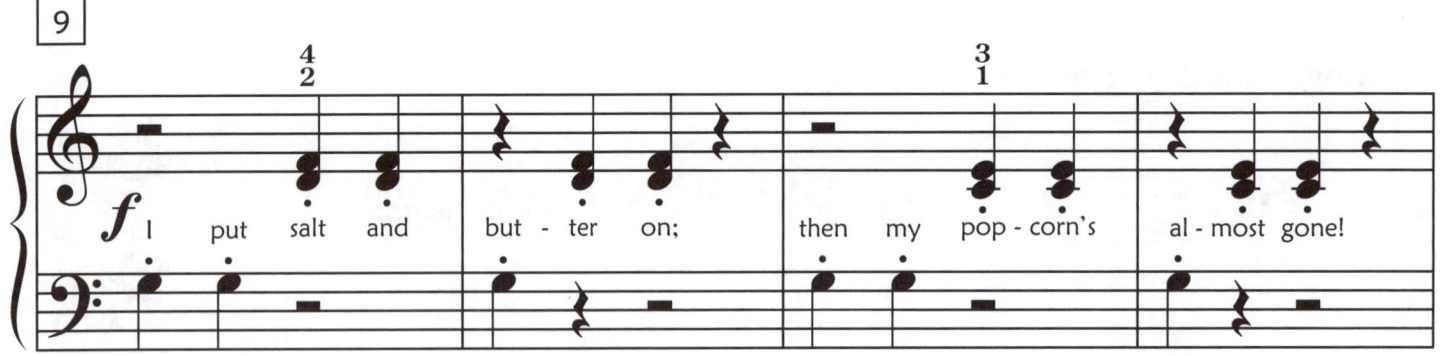

Move RH up · **RH 1 octave higher to end**

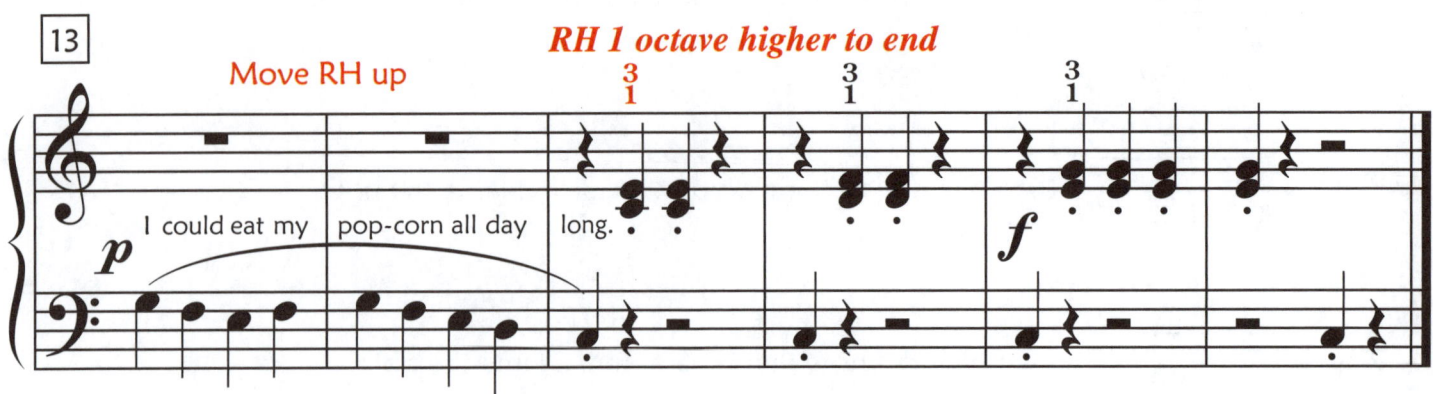

Performance Book: pages 10–11

Chopsticks

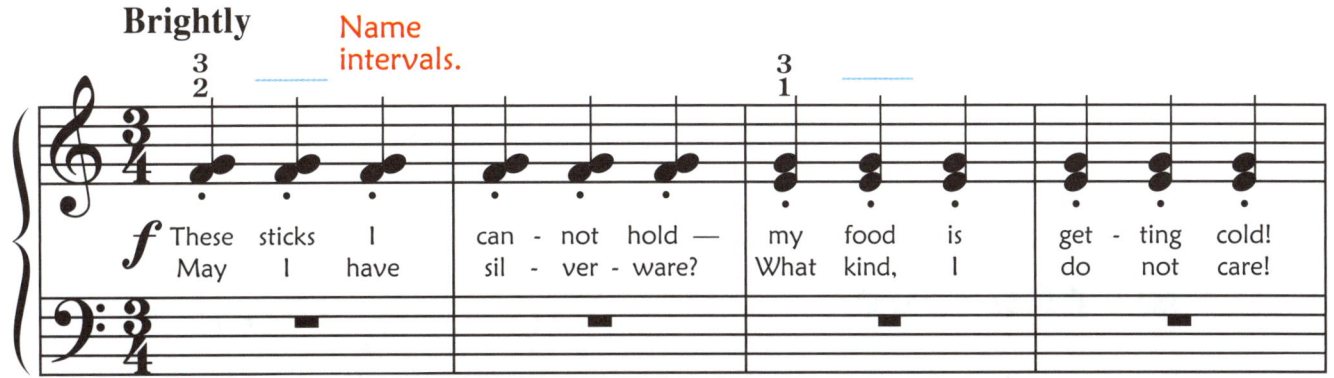

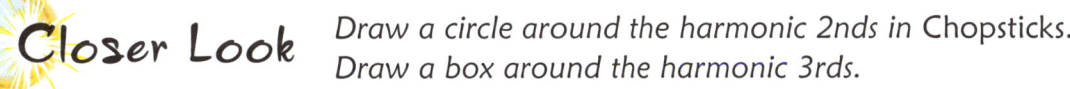 **Closer Look** — Draw a circle around the harmonic 2nds in Chopsticks. Draw a box around the harmonic 3rds.

Duet: Student plays one octave higher.

New Landmark Note

Treble C is written in the 3rd space of the treble stave.

Name two other C's you know.

_____ C

_____ C

Landmark Notes

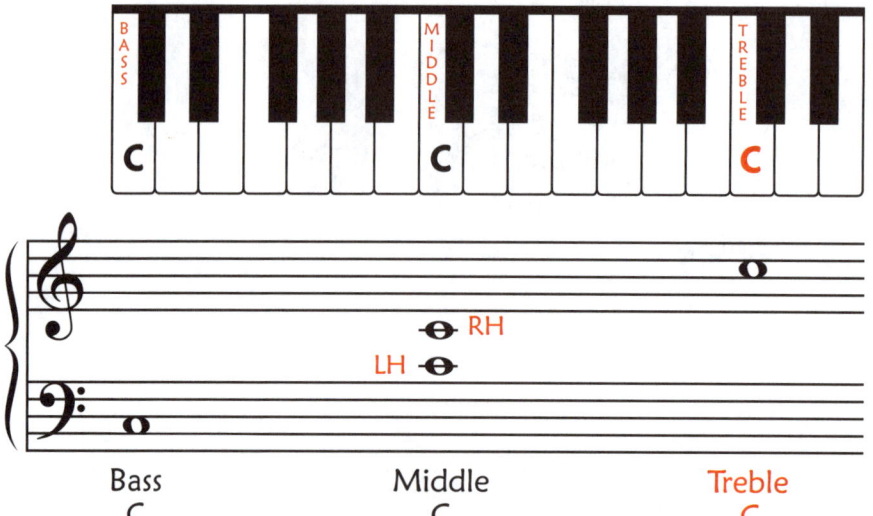

Bass C   Middle C   Treble C

C, Over and Over

Imagination Station

Using the 3 landmark C's, create your own piece.

Adapted from Tchaikovsky's *1812 Overture*

Duet (for 1 & 2)
CD 29/30
GM 15

Row, Row, Row Your Boat

CD 31/32   GM 16

Theory Book: page 22

Ritardando means to slow the tempo gradually. It is usually written ***rit.*** or ***ritard.***

Name interval. ____

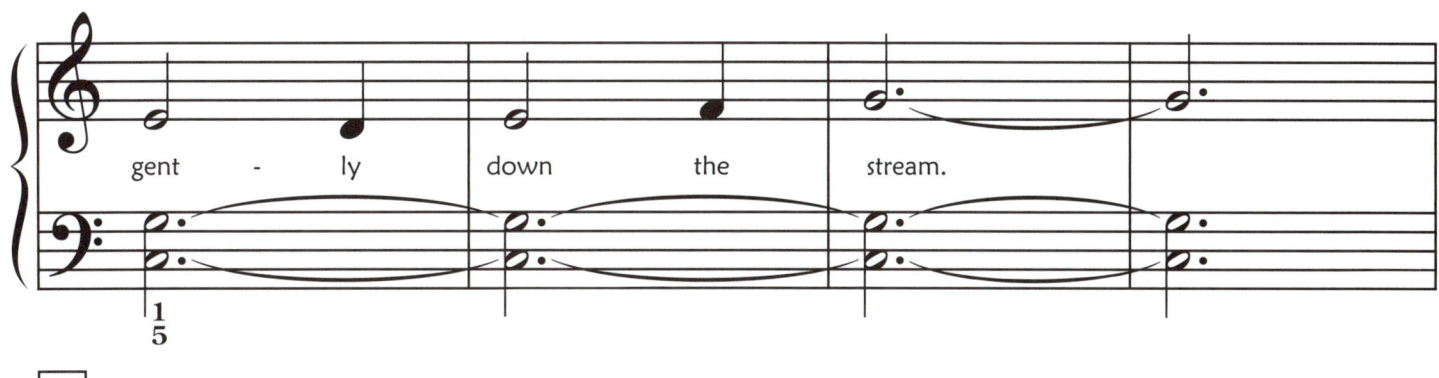

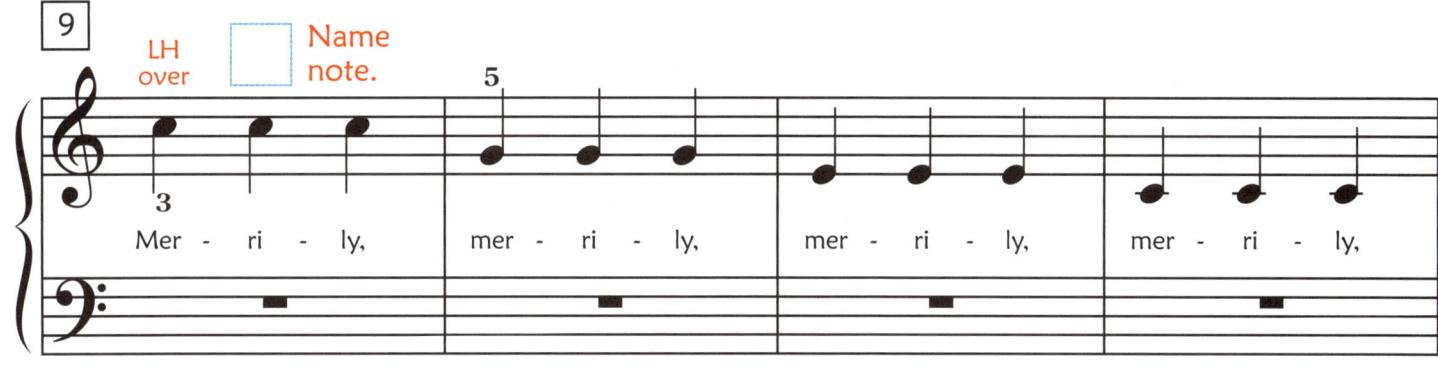

Name interval. ____

Press sustain pedal and hold to end.

Premier Performer

Play lines 1, 2 and 4 of Row, Row, Row Your Boat very legato.

Theory Book: page 23
Performance Book: page 13

New Notes B and D

2nds up and down from Treble C

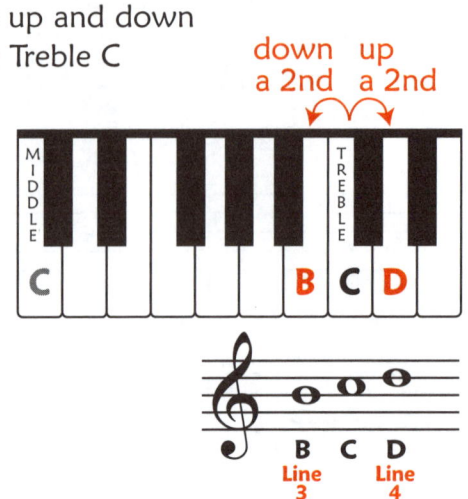

Sight-Reading

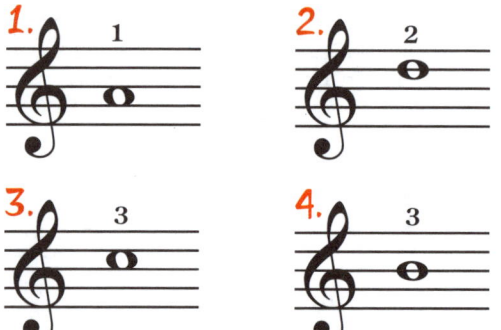

Play and say the note names as quickly as you can, 3 times each day. Use the correct fingering.

Picnic Ants

Like a march

Pic-nic blan-ket on the ground— it's the best spot in town till the ants be-gin to roam. Let's go home!

gradually louder

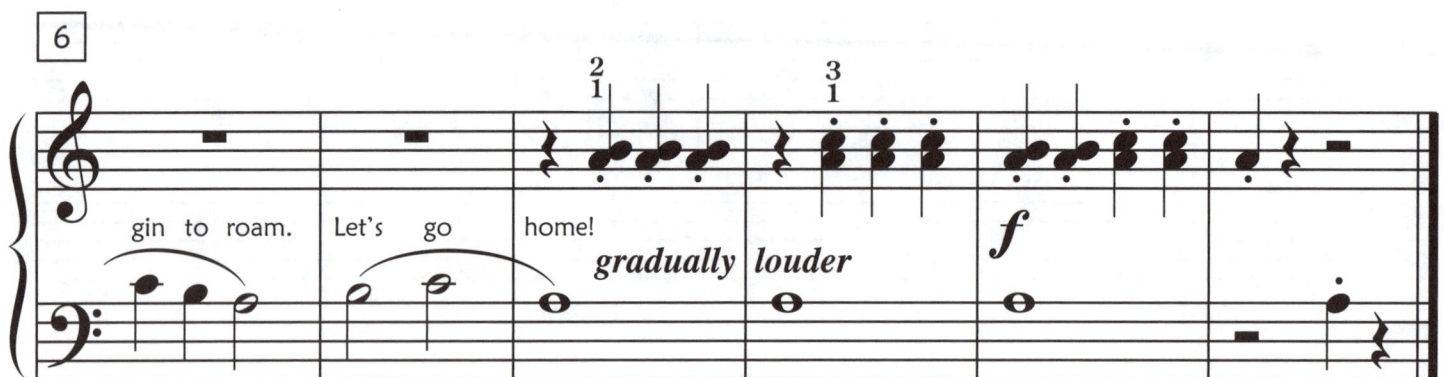

Duet: Student plays one octave higher.

Like a march

CD 33/34
GM 17

Theory Book: page 24
Performance Book: pages 14–15

Moving Up from Treble G

for the G 5-finger pattern

Treble G and the four notes that step up from it are called the *G 5-finger pattern.*

Stepping Up—2nds

RH 1 2 3 4 5
G A B C D
2nd 2nd 2nd 2nd

Skipping Up—3rds

RH 1 3 5
G B D
3rd 3rd

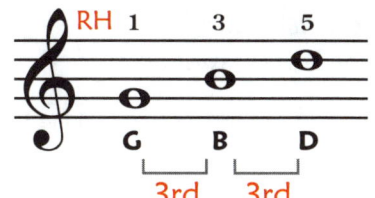

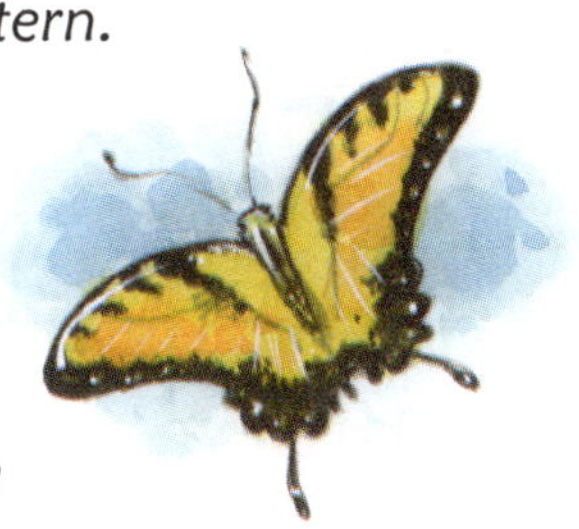

- Starting with Treble G, point to each note as you say its name.
- Play with the RH and say the note names.

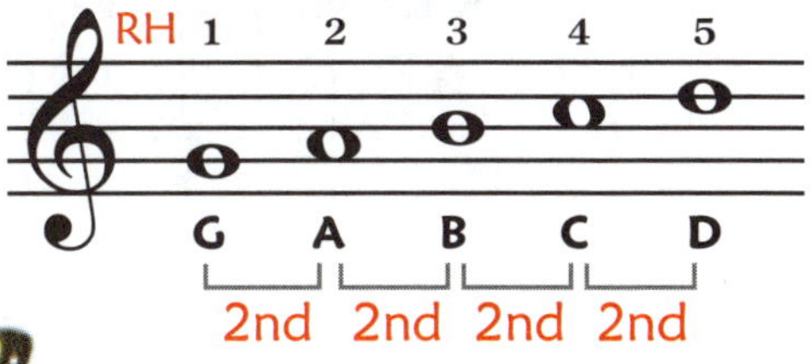

Butterfly

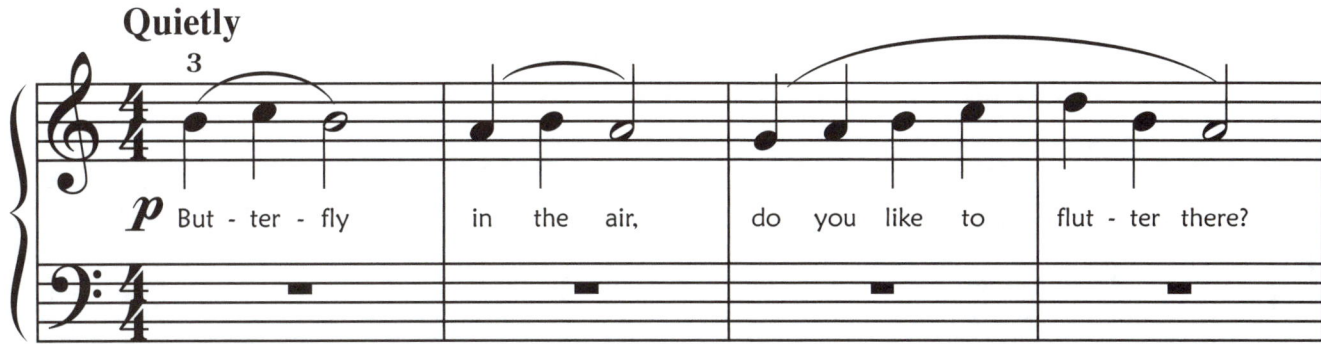

Quietly
p
But - ter - fly in the air, do you like to flut - ter there?
5
May-be you would rath - er be sit - ting on the grass with me,
rit.
rest - ing on my knee.

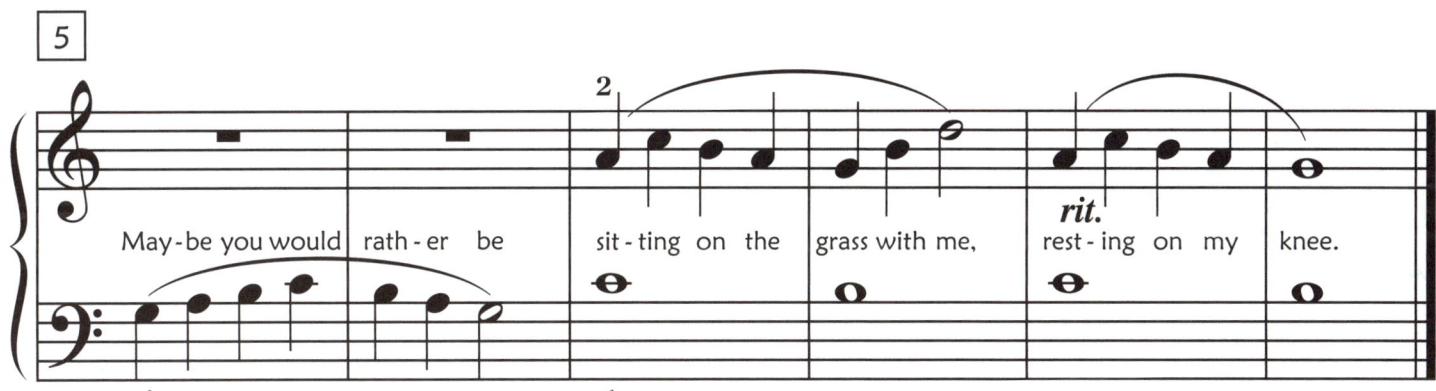

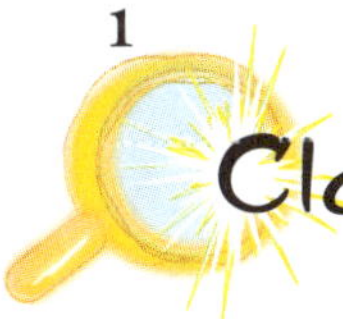

Closer Look *Circle the symbol in* Butterfly *that tells you to slow down gradually.*

Duet: Student plays one octave higher.

Quietly
CD 35/36
GM 18
RH
LH
pp
5
rit.

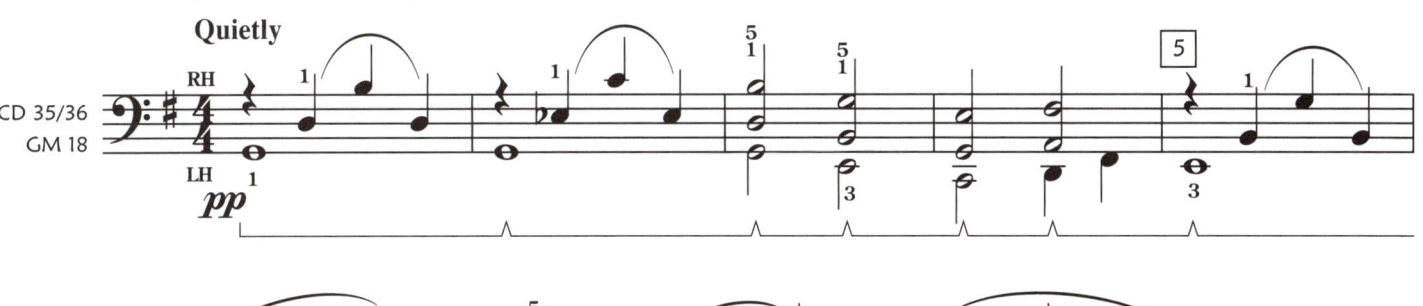

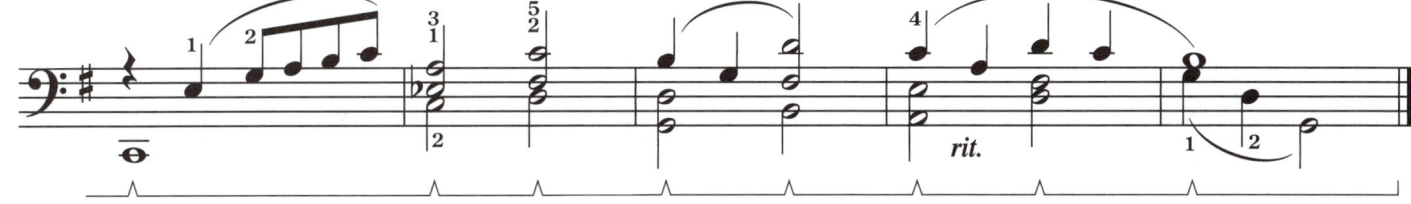

New Landmark Note

Low G is written on the 1st line of the bass stave.

Name two other G's you know.

_____ G

_____ G

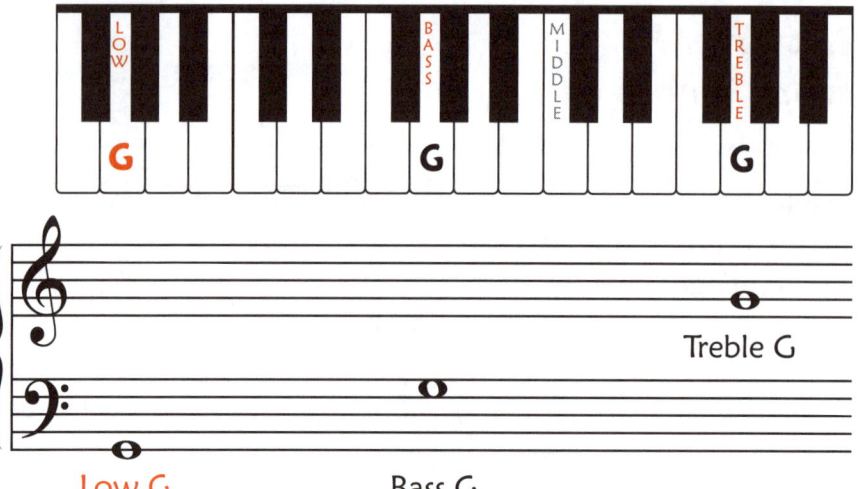

G, Over and Over

Imagination Station

Using the 3 landmark G's, create your own piece.

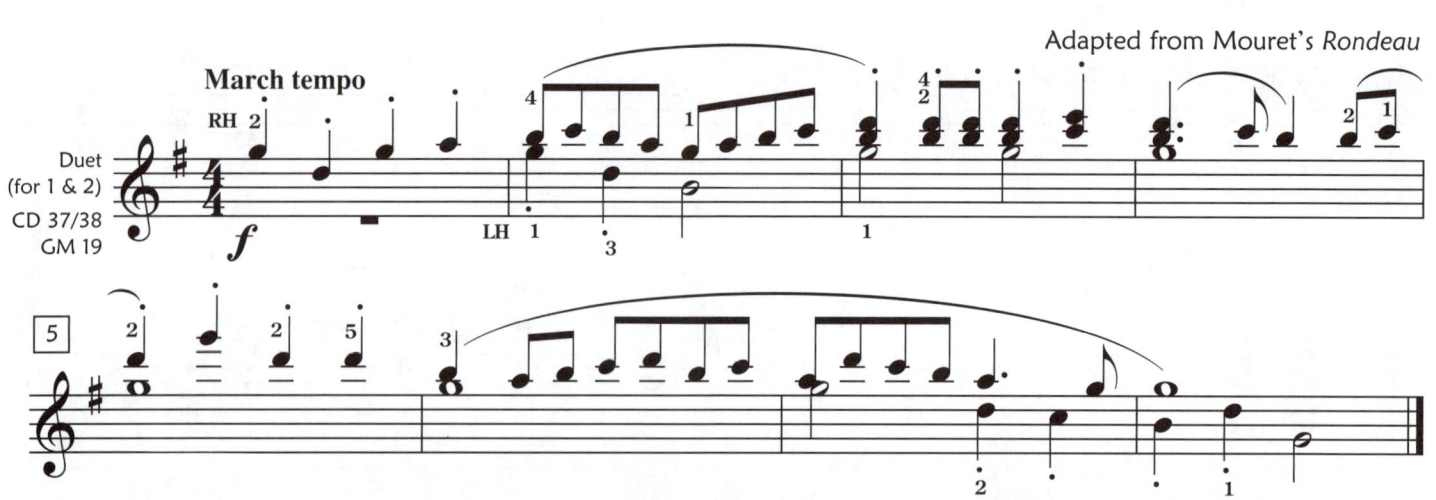

Adapted from Mouret's *Rondeau*

New Notes A and B

A 2nd and 3rd up from Low G

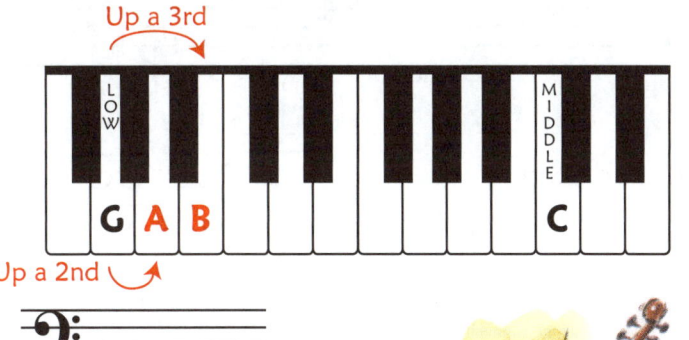

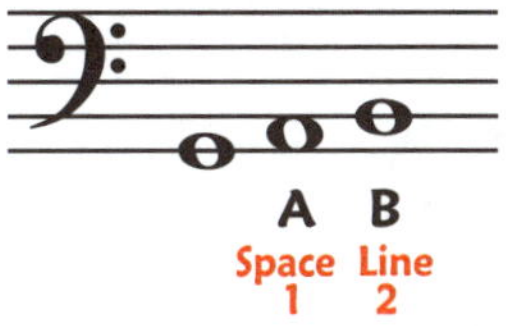

Symphony Hall

CD 39/40 GM 20

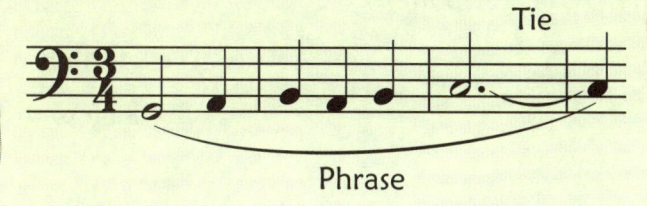

> A **phrase** is a group of notes similar to a sentence. It expresses a musical idea. A longer **slur** (called a phrase mark) is used to show a phrase. Phrases are usually played *legato*.

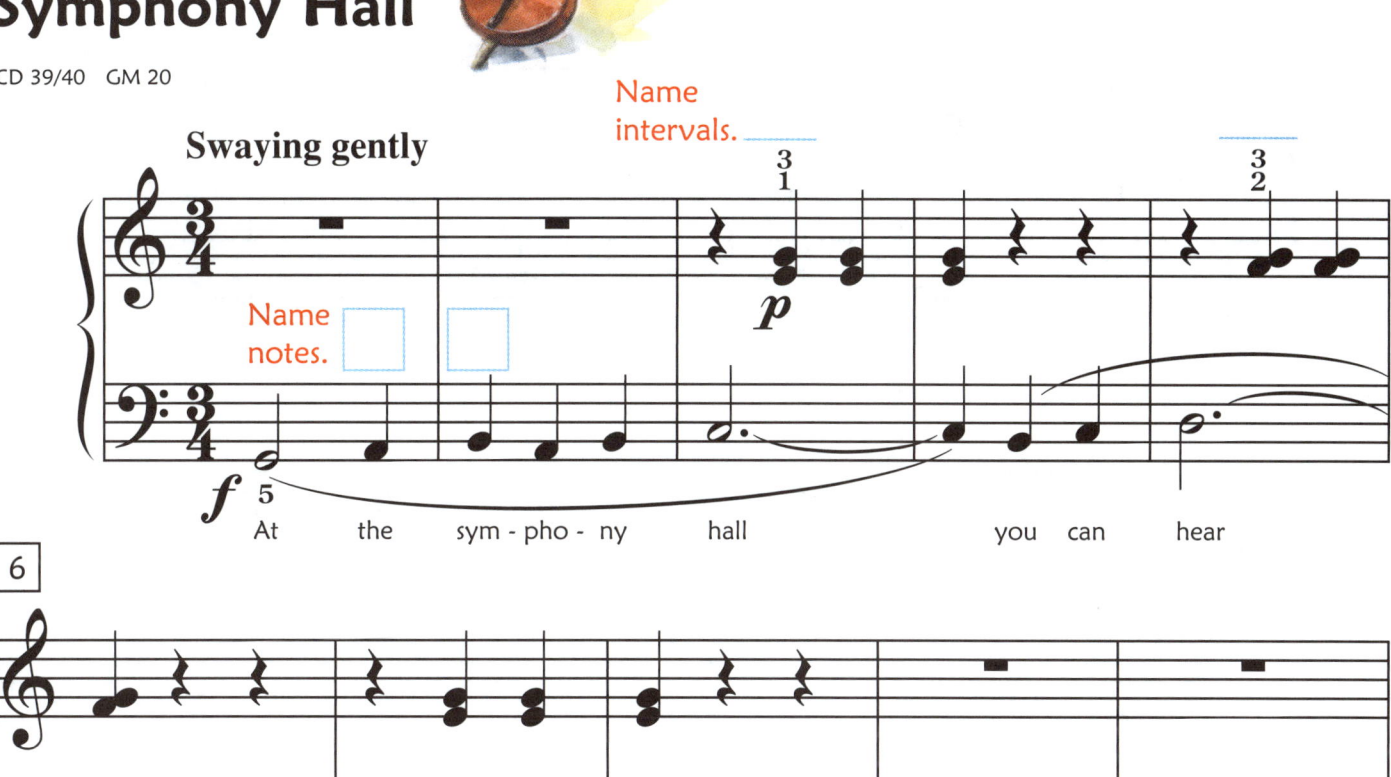
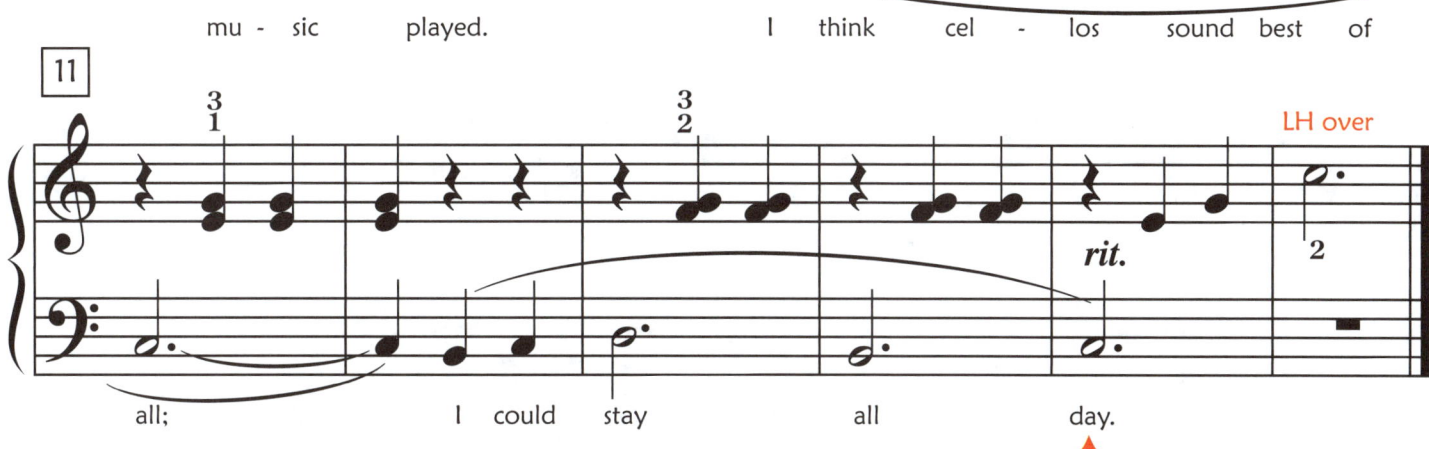

Press sustain pedal and hold to end.

Theory Book: pages 26–27

Theory Book: page 28

Moving Up from Low G

for the G 5-finger pattern

Low G and the four notes that step up from it are called the *G 5-finger pattern*.

Stepping Up—2nds

LH 5 4 3 2 1
G A B C D
2nd 2nd 2nd 2nd

Skipping Up—3rds

LH 5 3 1
G B D
3rd 3rd

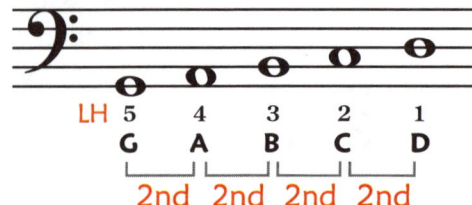

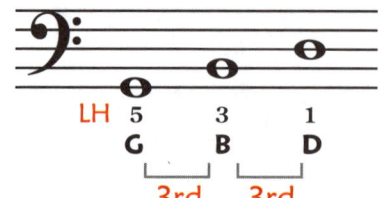

- Starting with Low G, point to each note as you say its name.
- Play with the LH and say the note names.

Sara's Musette

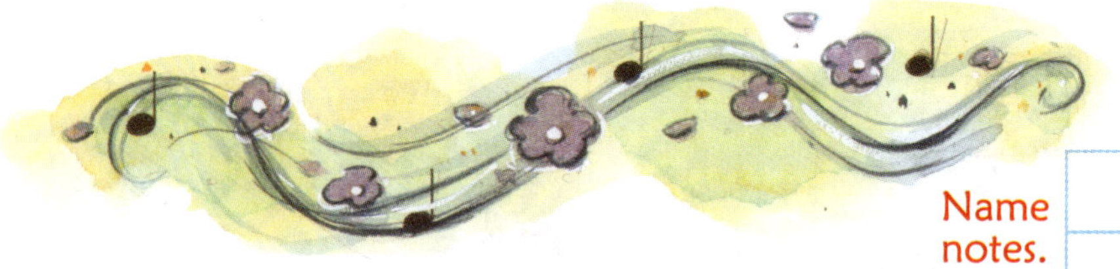

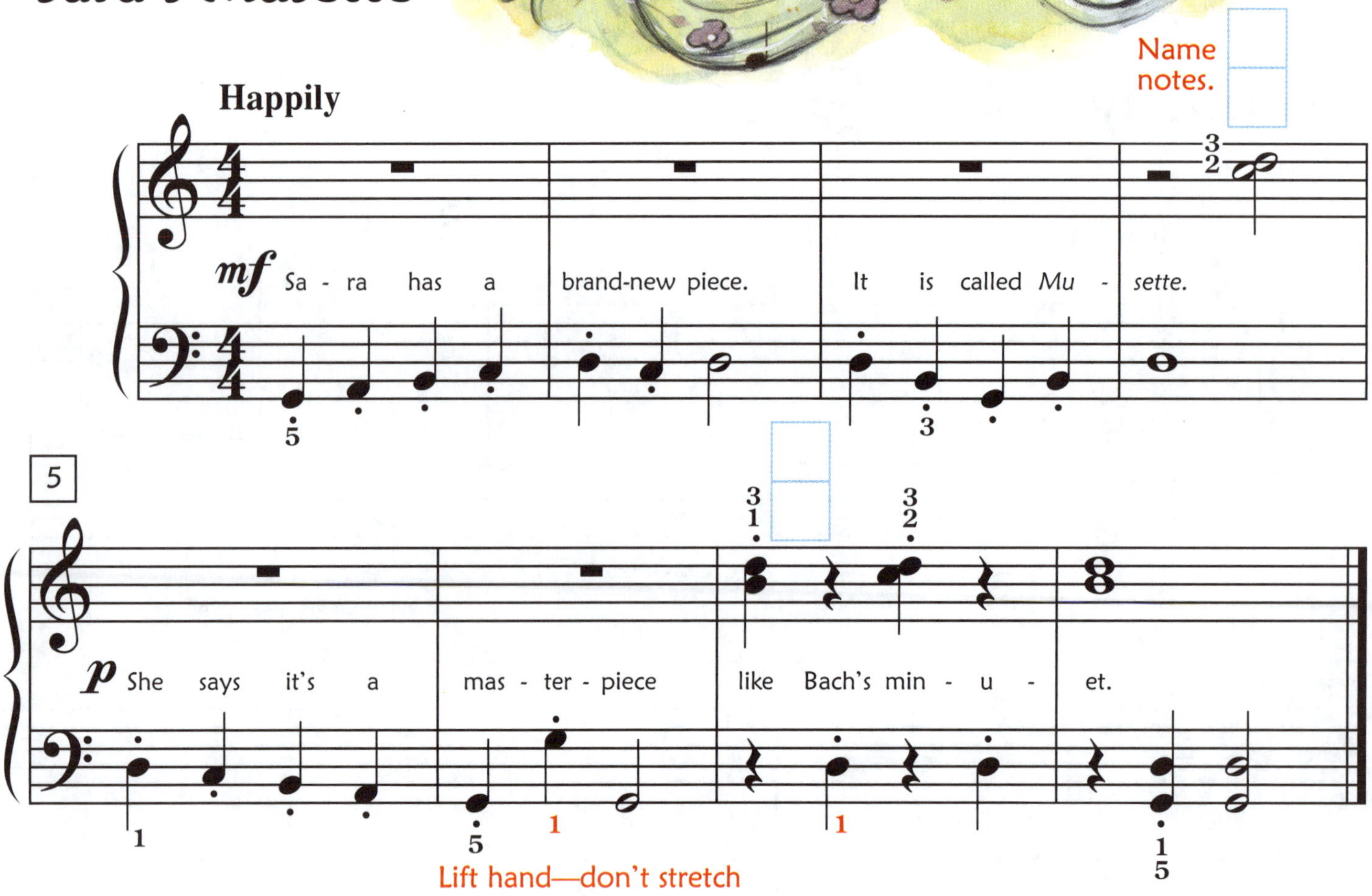

Name notes.
Happily
mf
Sa - ra has a brand-new piece. It is called Mu - sette.
p
She says it's a mas - ter - piece like Bach's min - u - et.
Lift hand—don't stretch

Duet: Student plays **RH** one octave **lower.**

Adapted from J. S. Bach's *Musette in D*

Happily
RH
LH
mp
pp
CD 41/42
GM 21

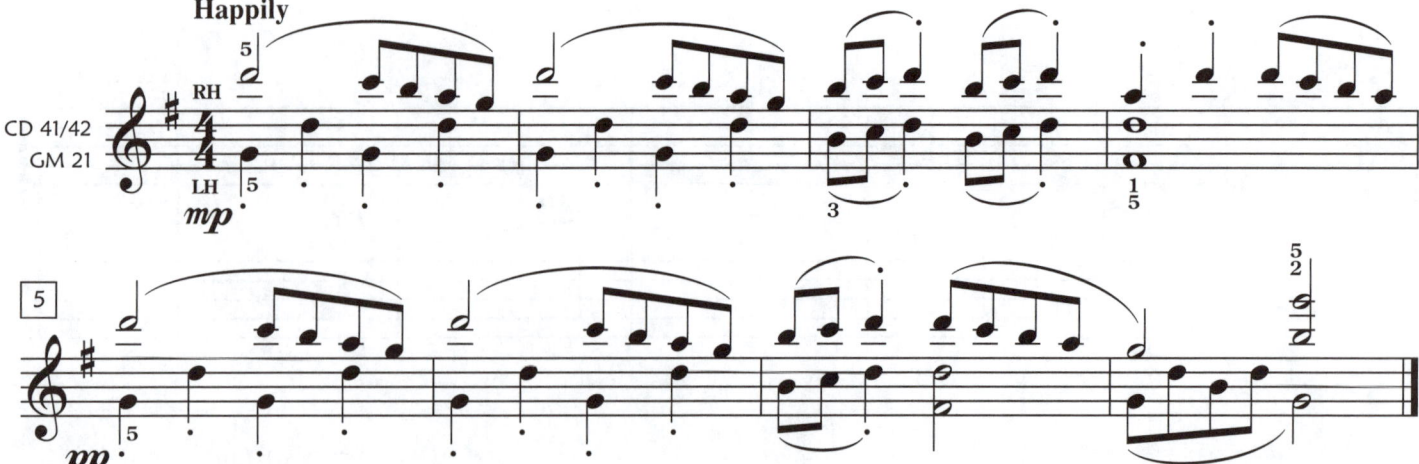

Theory Book: page 29
Performance Book: pages 16–17

8va

When placed *above* the stave, *8va* means to play one octave (8 notes) higher than written.

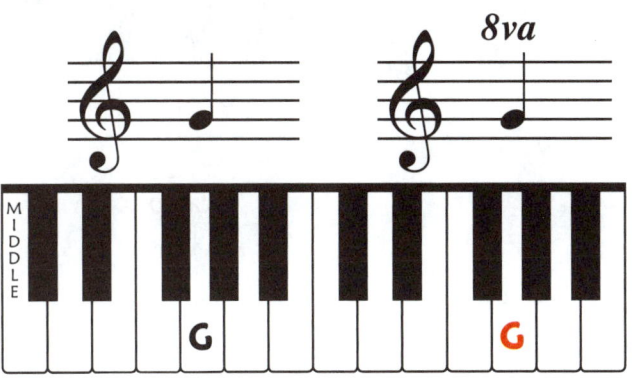

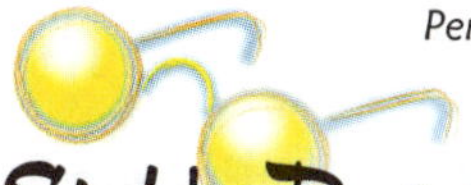

Sight-Reading

Play and say the note names as quickly as you can, 3 times each day. Use the correct fingering.

1.

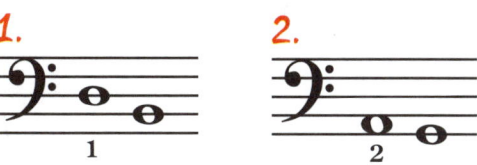

2.

3.

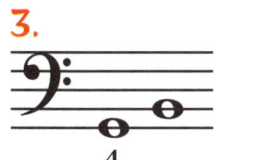

4.

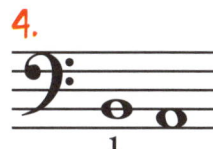

My Yo-Yo

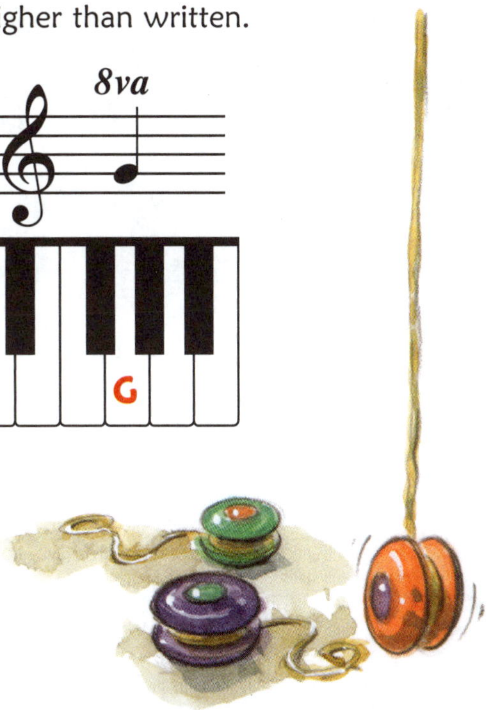

CD 43/44 GM 22

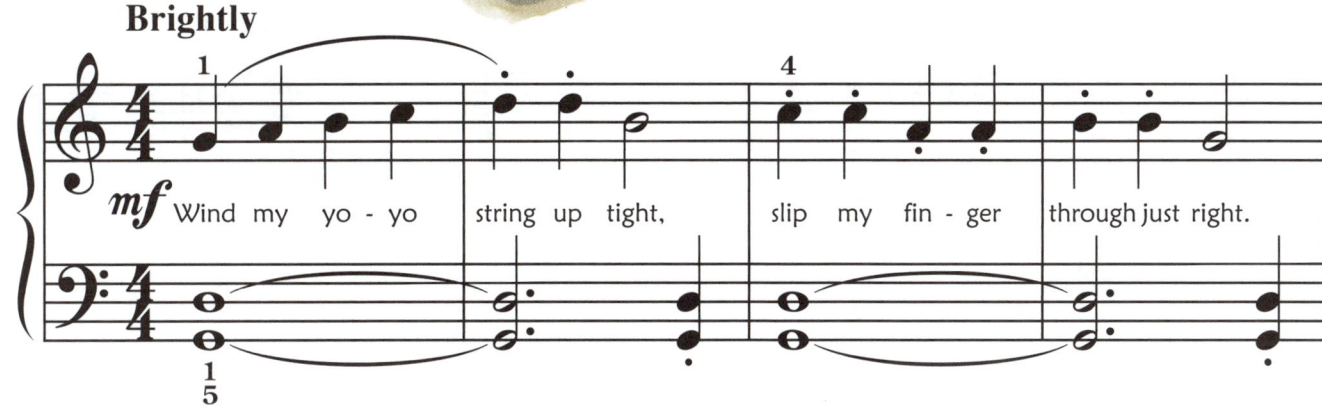

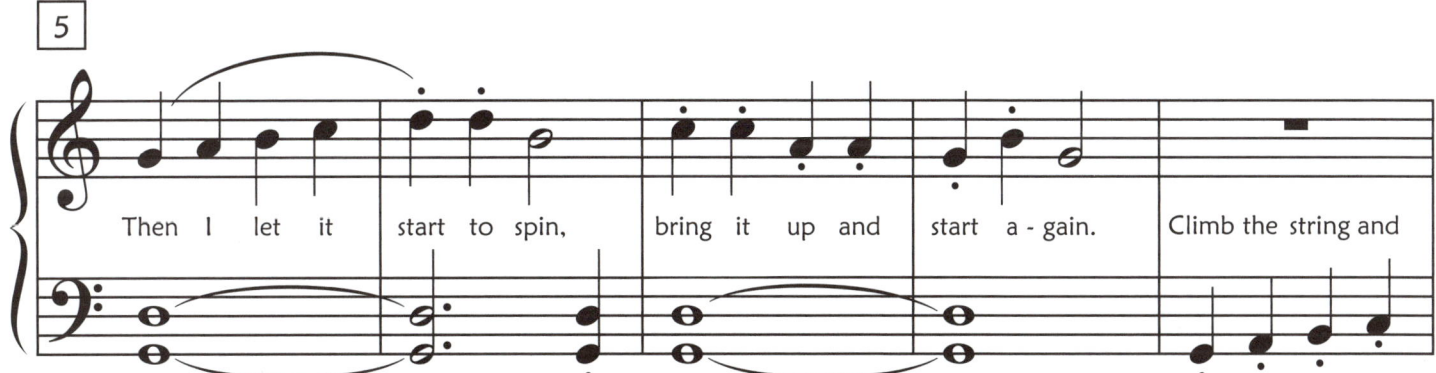

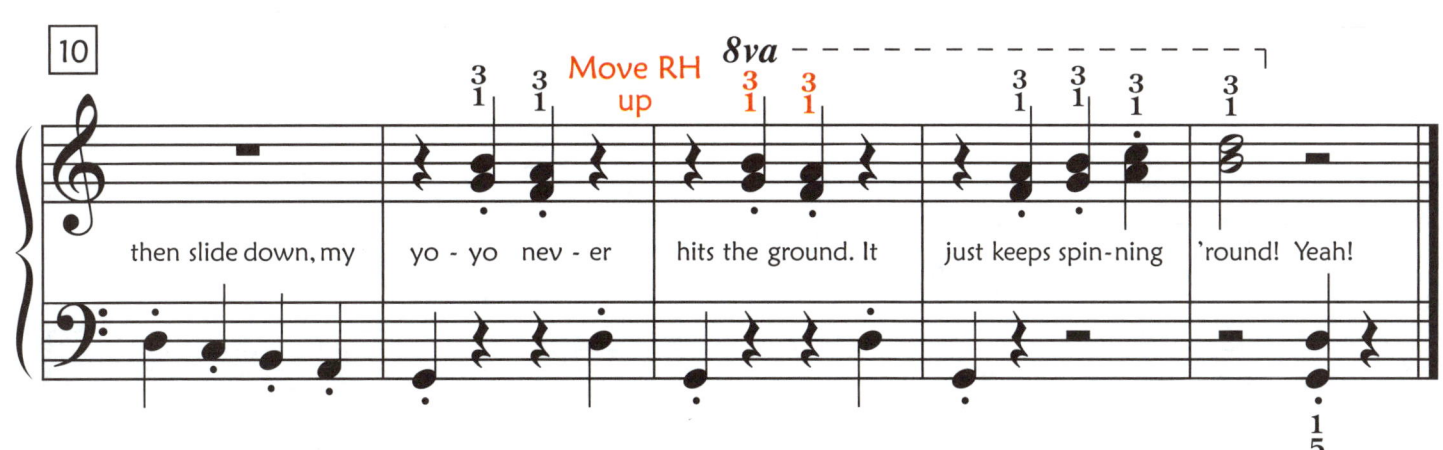

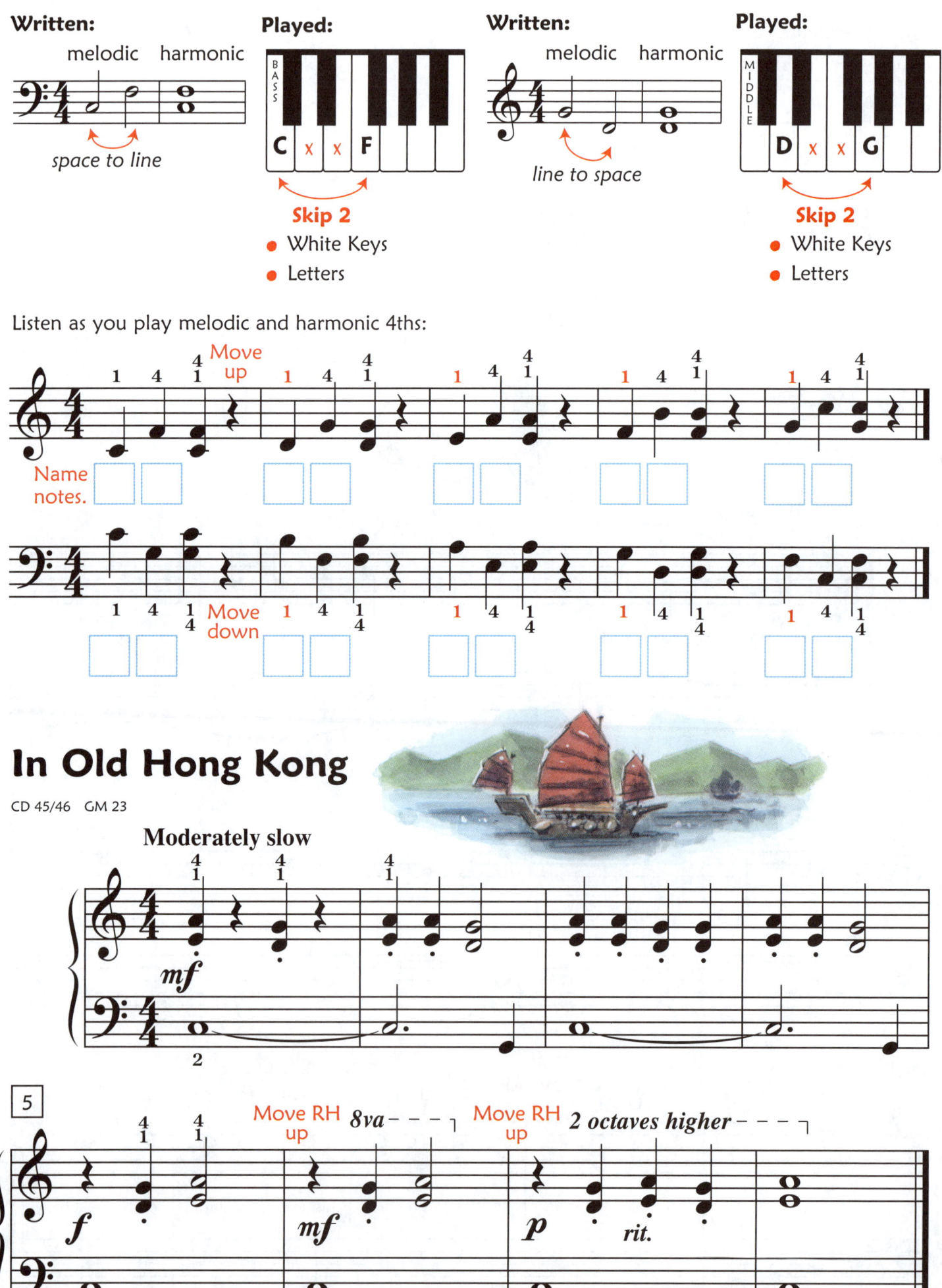

Theory Book: page 31
Performance Book: page 18

Workout 6 Hands Together

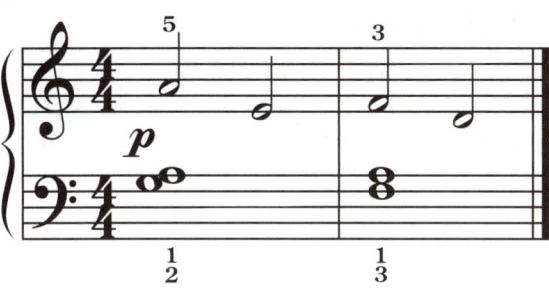

Play 3 times each day.

Rhythm Review

Count: 1 – 2 – 3 4 1 2 3 – 4

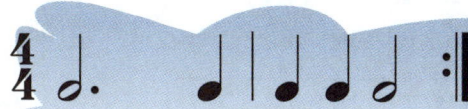

Tap and count the rhythm.

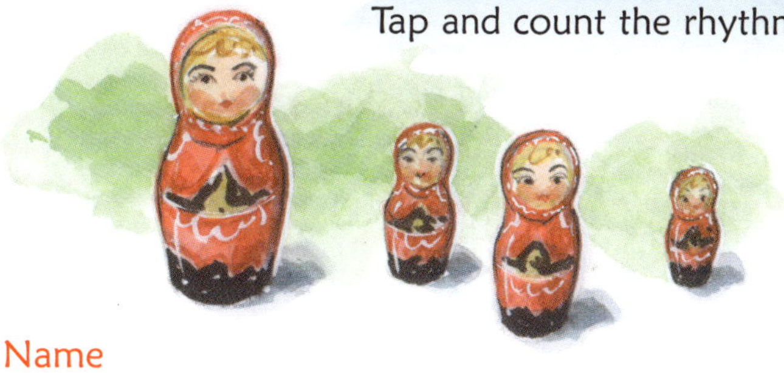

Russian Folk Tale

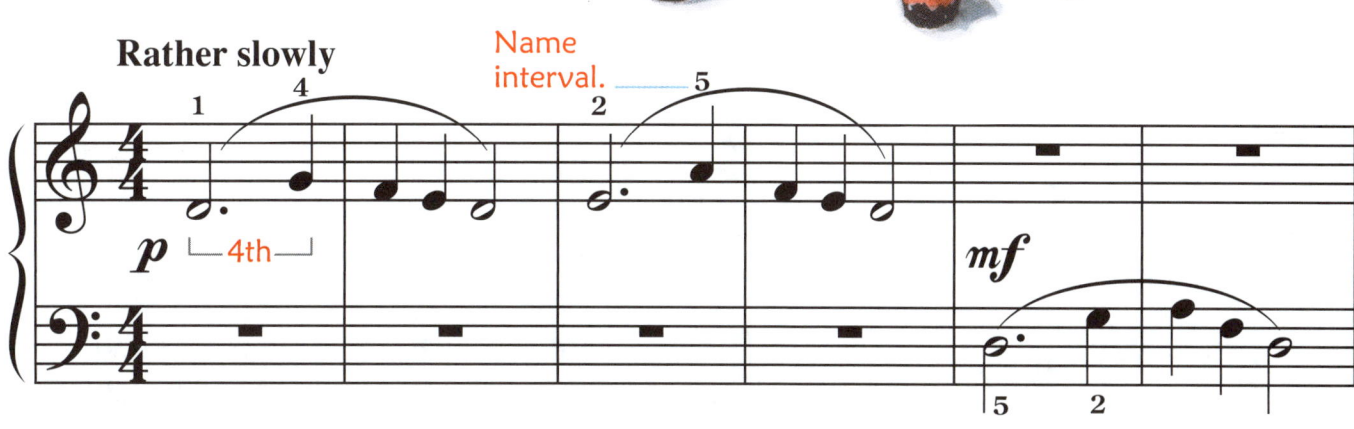

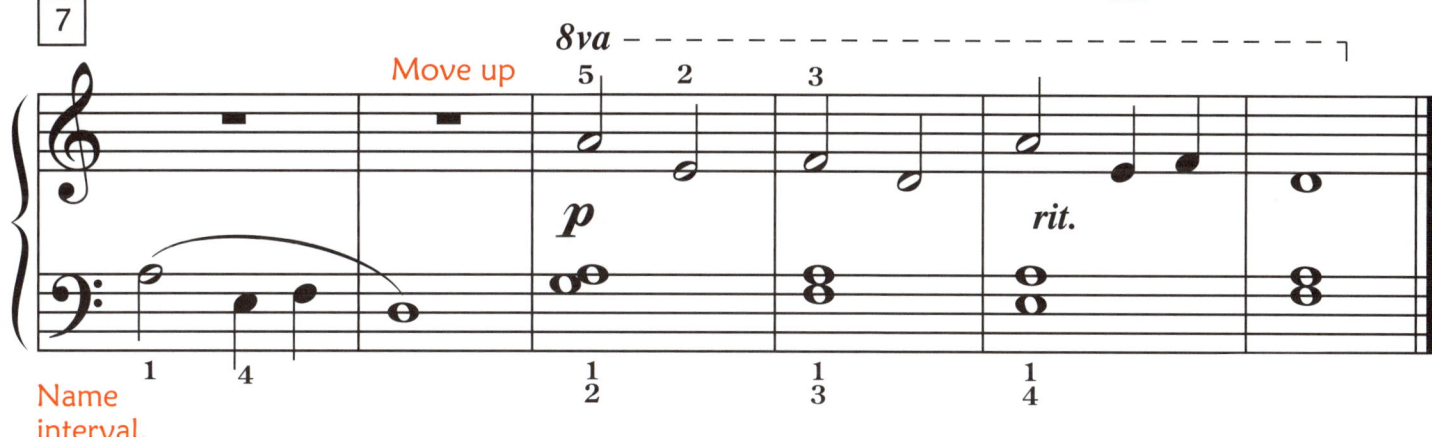

Duet: Student plays one octave higher.

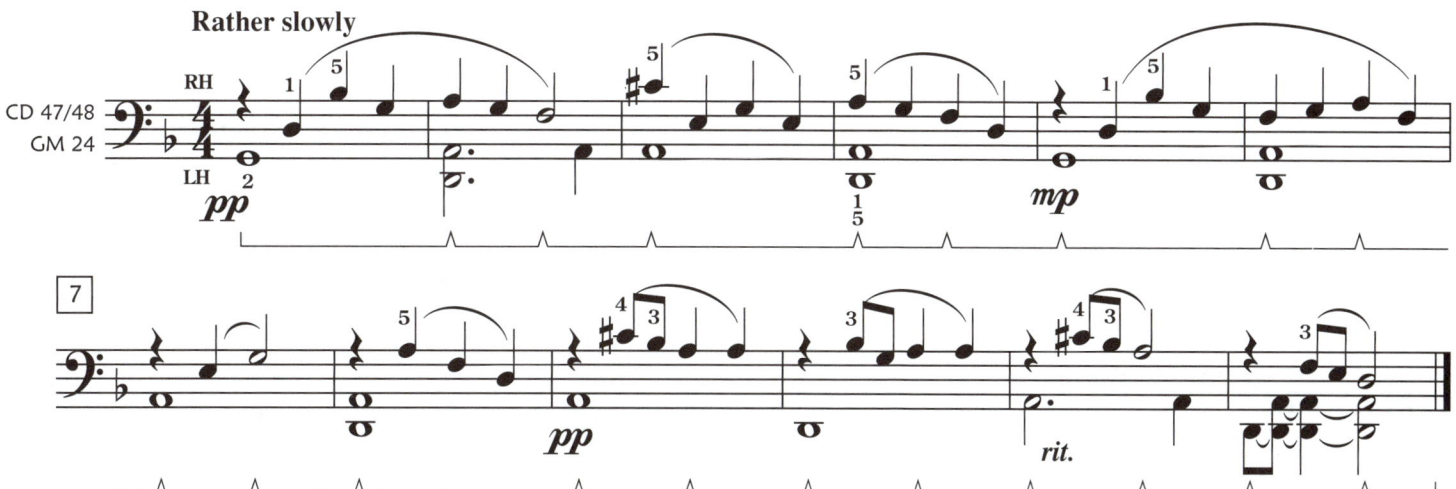

Interval of a 5th

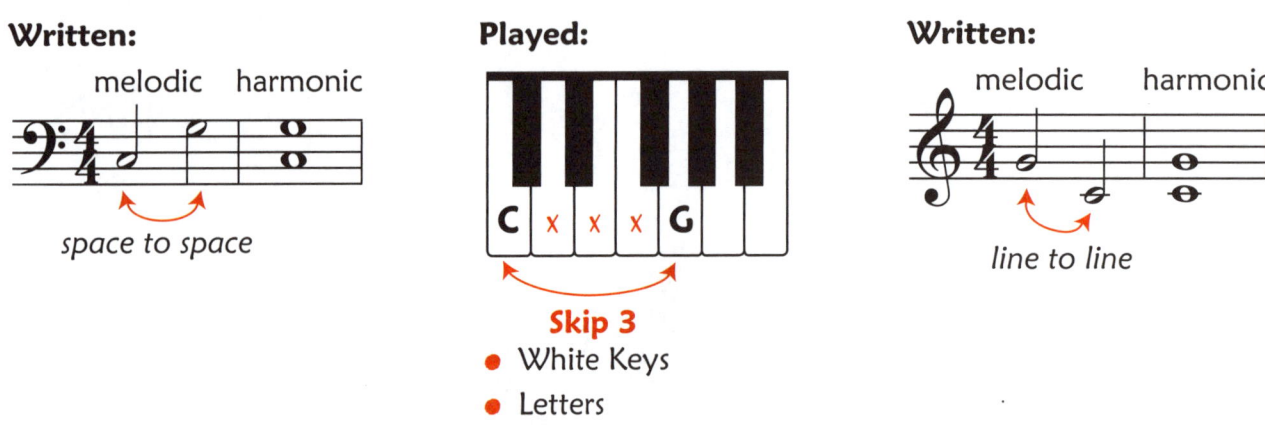

Listen as you play melodic and harmonic 5ths:

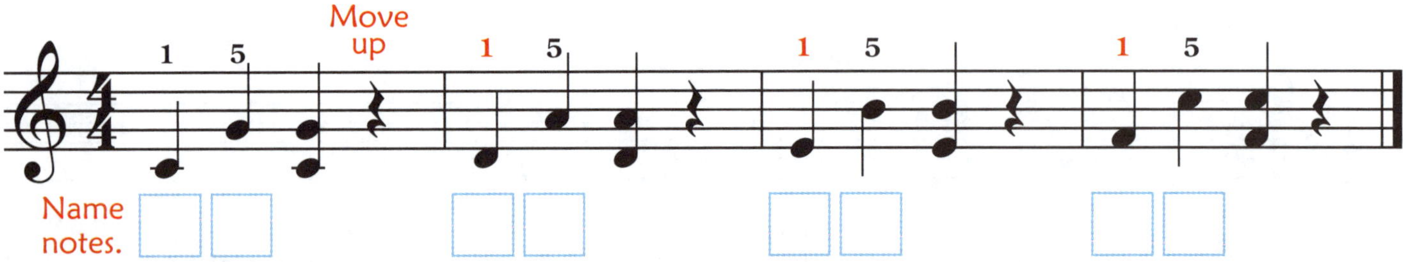

Name notes.

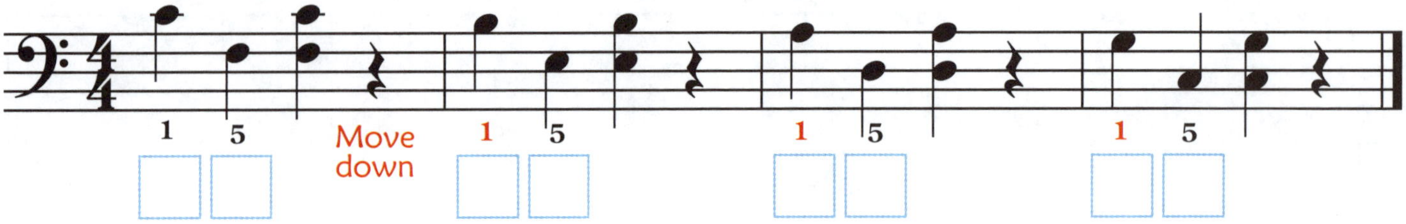

Wind Chimes

CD 49/50   GM 25

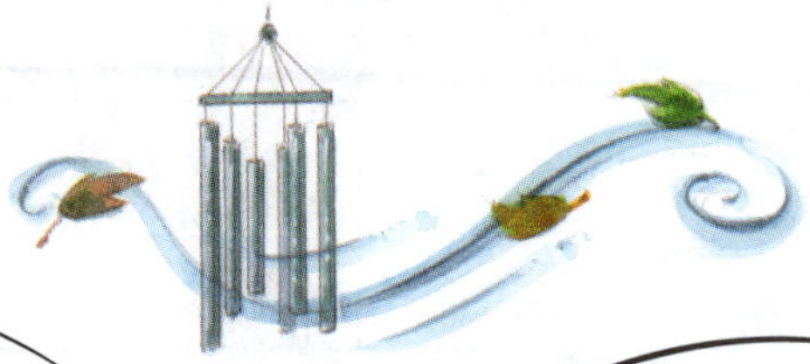

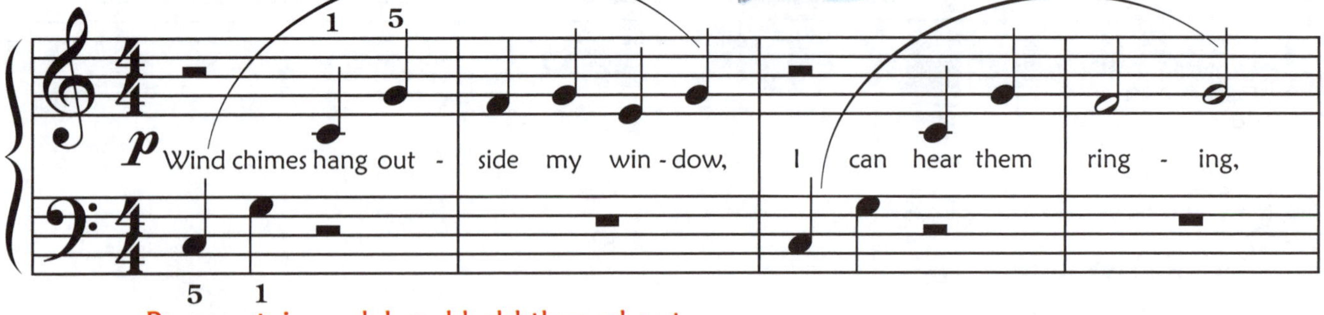

Press sustain pedal and hold throughout.

gradually louder to end

Play both hands 8va on repeat

The Bells of St. Joseph

CD 51/52   GM 26

A **fermata** over or under a note means to hold the note longer than its rhythmic value.

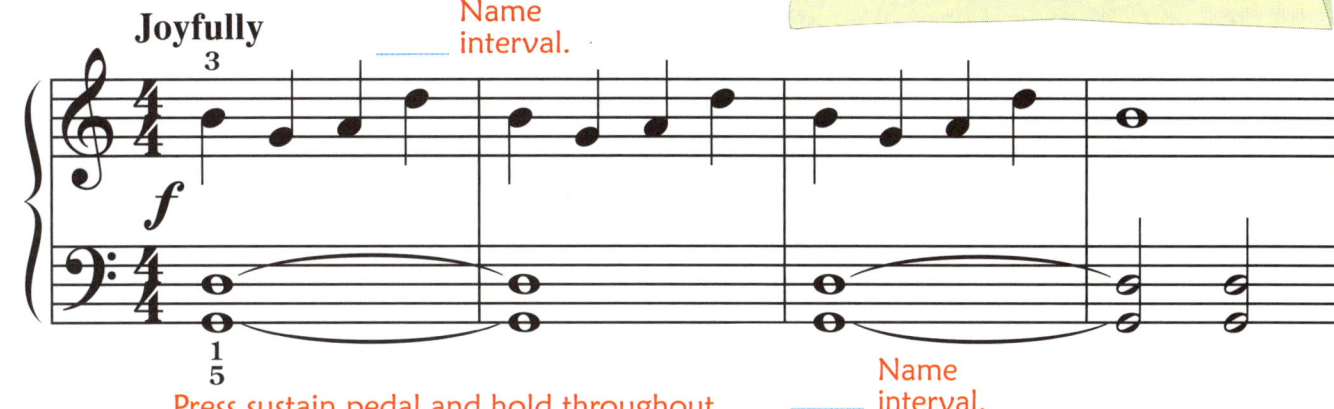

Press sustain pedal and hold throughout.

gradually softer to end

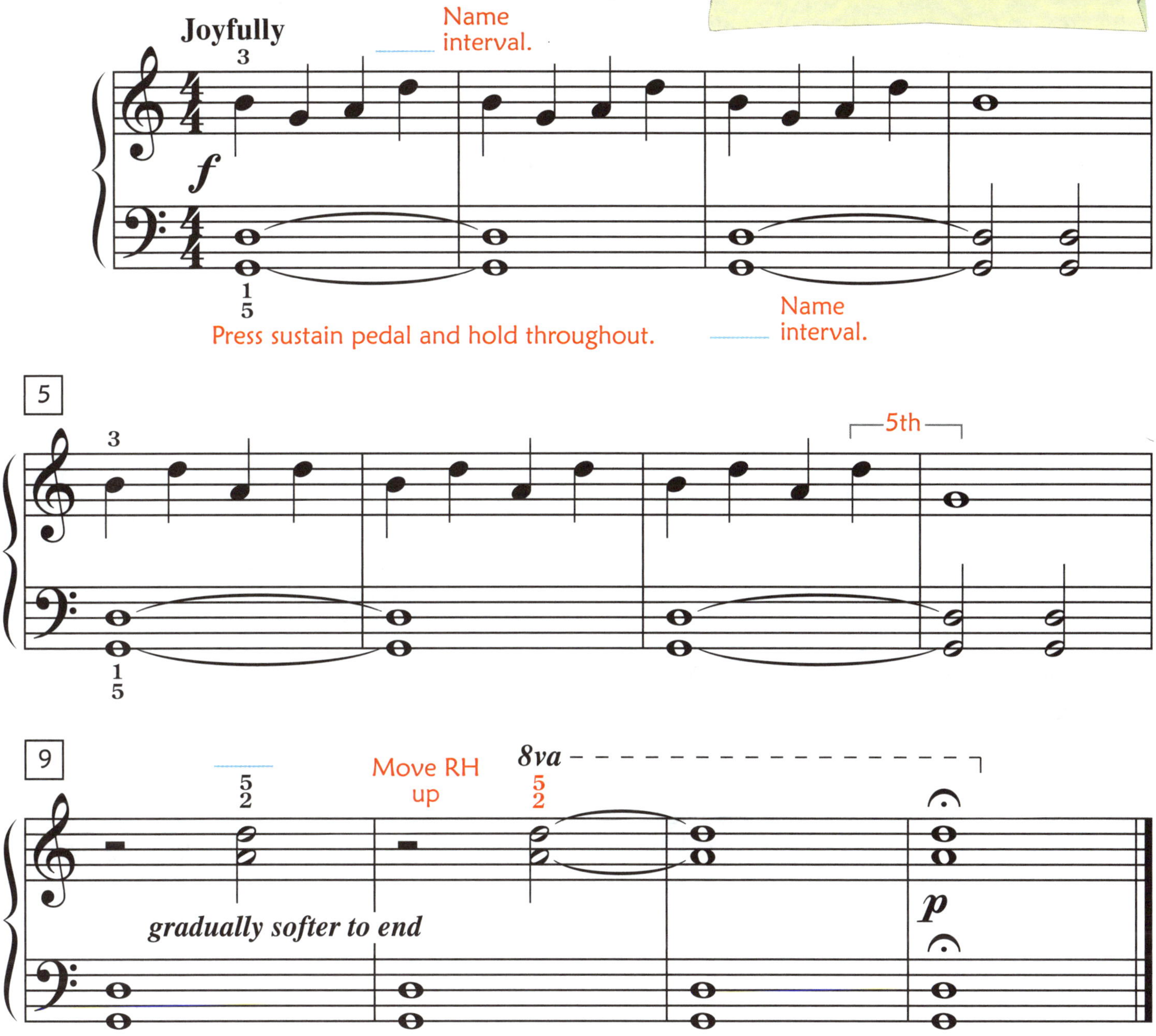

Premier Performer

Remember to play The Bells of St. Joseph with level wrists and strong fingertips.

Finding 4ths and 5ths

a. Play  then play the note that is *up* a 5th. Name the note. ____

b. Play  then play the note that is *up* a 4th. Name the note. ____

c. Play  then play the note that is *down* a 4th. Name the note. ____

d. Play  then play the note that is *down* a 5th. Name the note. ____

Theory Book: page 34

Moving Up a Semitone

The smallest interval on the keyboard is a **semitone.**

When moving *up* the keyboard, a semitone is the very next key to the *right*, black or white.

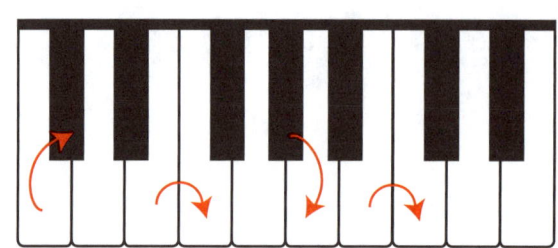

Circle one

- Play F, then the key a semitone higher. **black key** **white key**
- Play C, then the key a semitone higher. **black key** **white key**
- Play E, then the key a semitone higher. **black key** **white key**
- Play G, then the key a semitone higher. **black key** **white key**
- Play B, then the key a semitone higher. **black key** **white key**

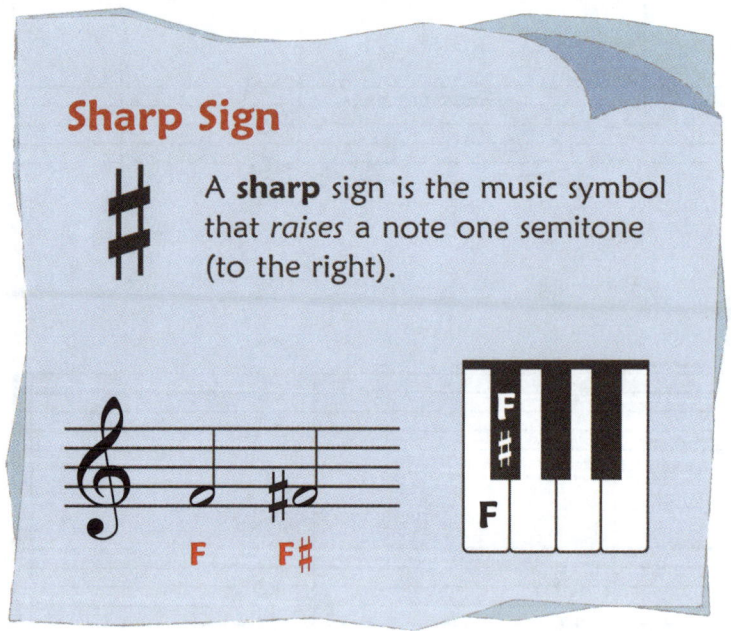

Sharp Sign

♯ A **sharp** sign is the music symbol that *raises* a note one semitone (to the right).

Sight-Reading

Play and say the note names as quickly as you can, 3 times each day.
Use the correct fingering.

1.

2.

3.

4.

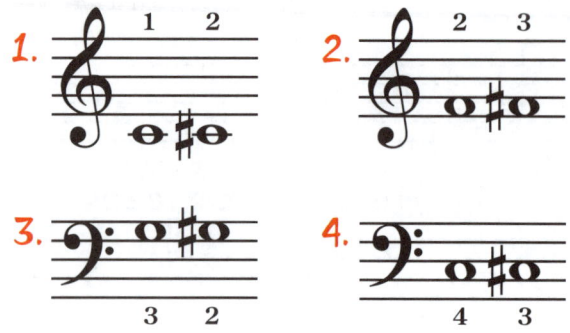

Write the name of each sharp key marked with an X. Note: E♯ and B♯ are white keys.

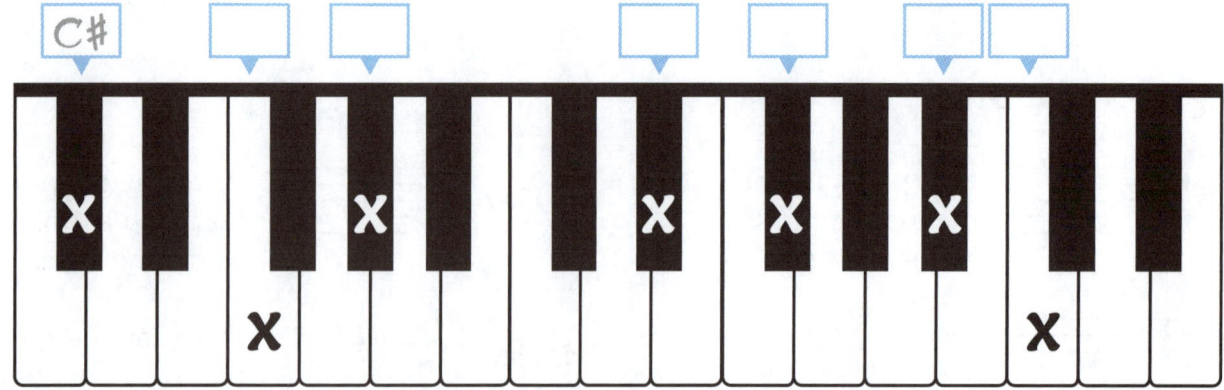

Hot Air Balloon

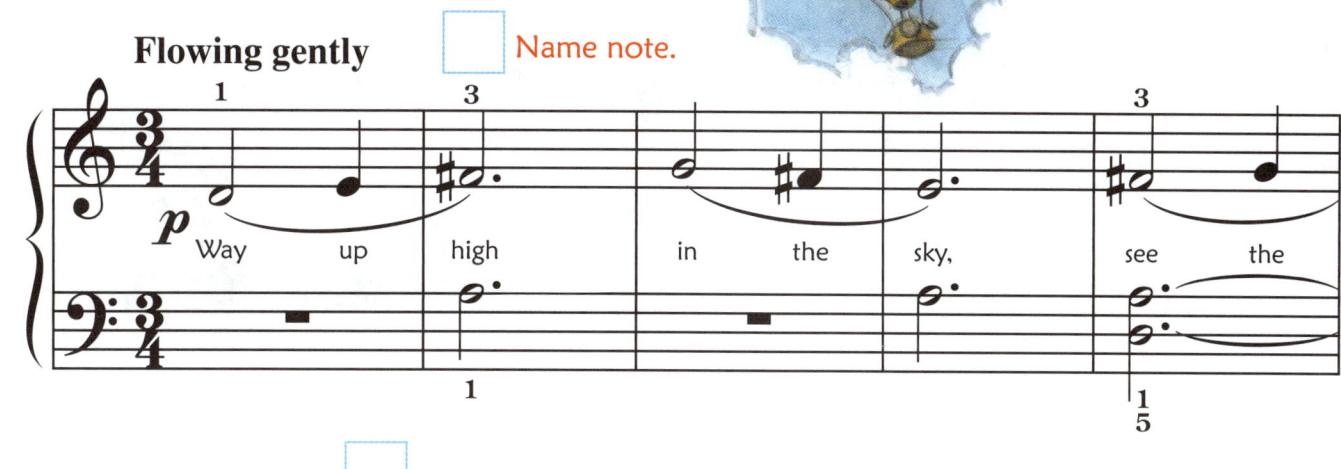
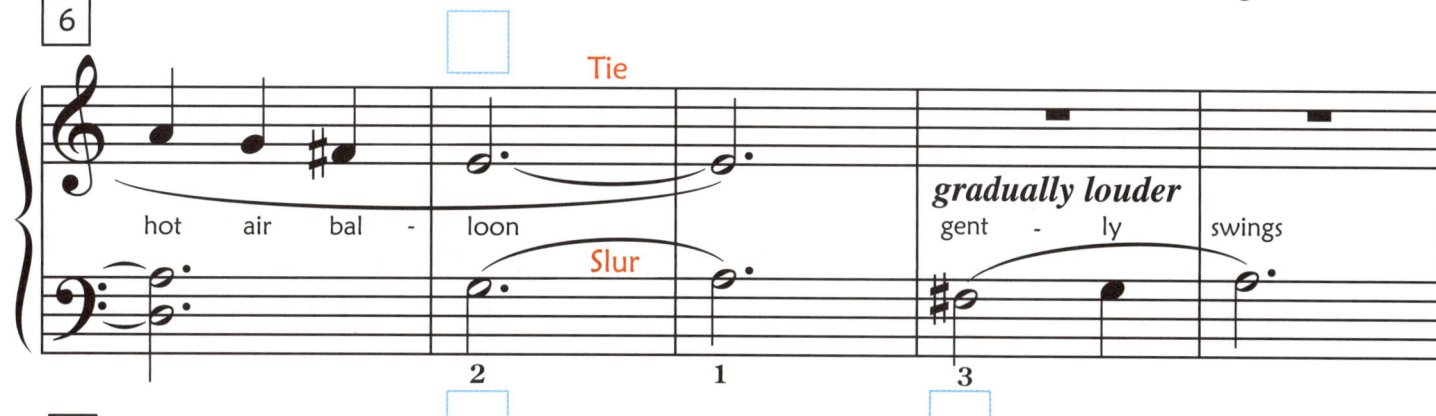

Duet: Student plays one octave higher.

A sharp applies to the same note for the rest of the bar.
The sharp sign is cancelled by the bar line at the end of the bar.

Creepy Crawler

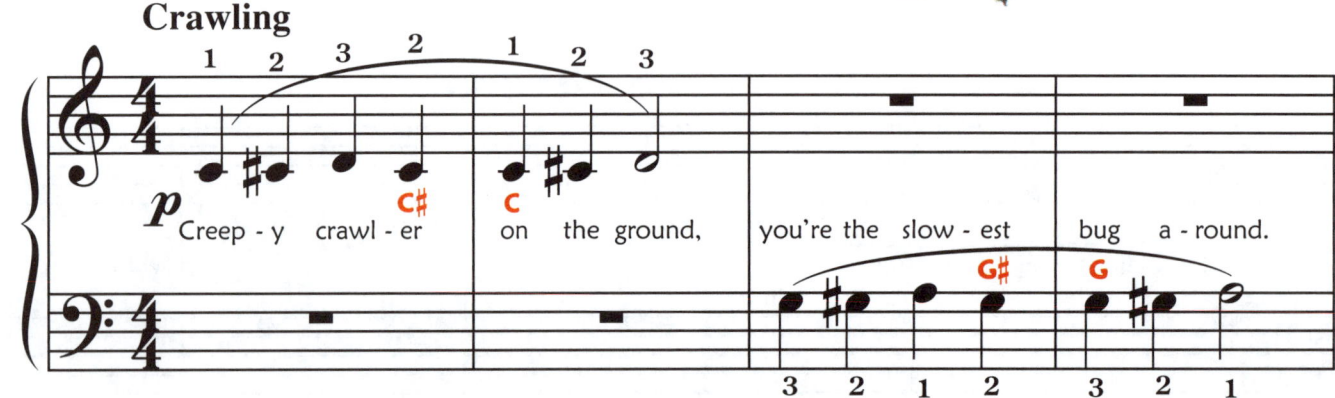

Premier Performer — Play Creepy Crawler *again and make every crotchet staccato.*

Duet: Student plays one octave higher.

Incomplete Bar

Some pieces of music begin and end with an **incomplete bar.**

- The first and last bars have fewer beats than shown by the time signature.
- The combined beats of both bars equal one full bar.
- The first note is called an *upbeat* or *pick-up* note.

I Asked My Mother

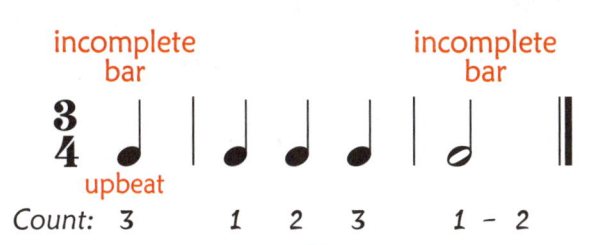

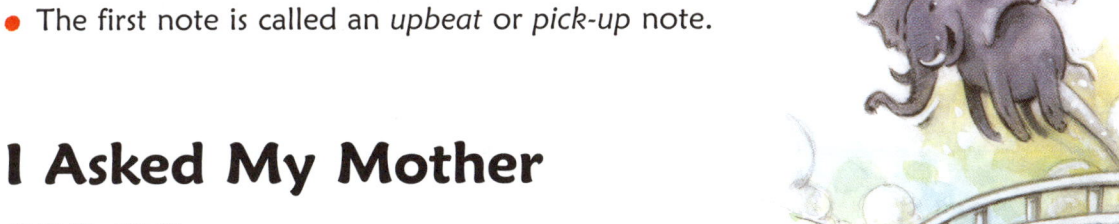

CD 57/58   GM 29

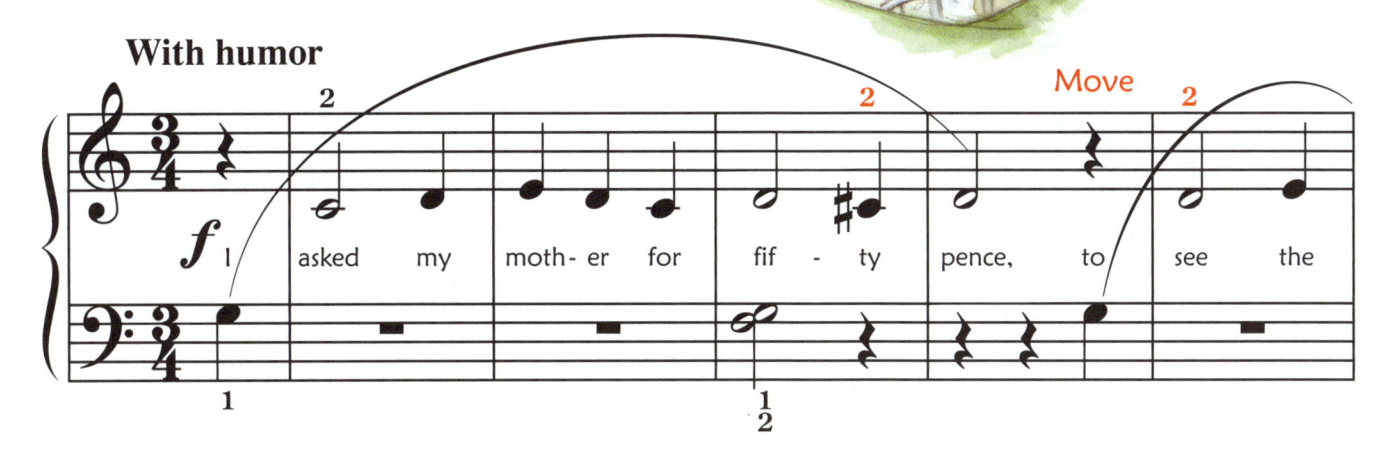

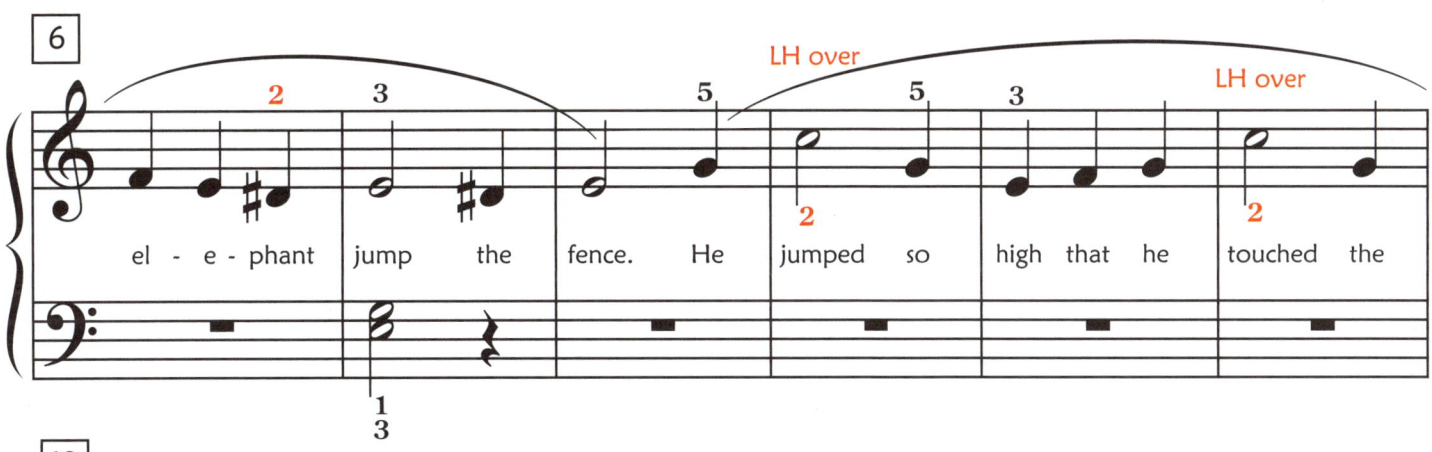

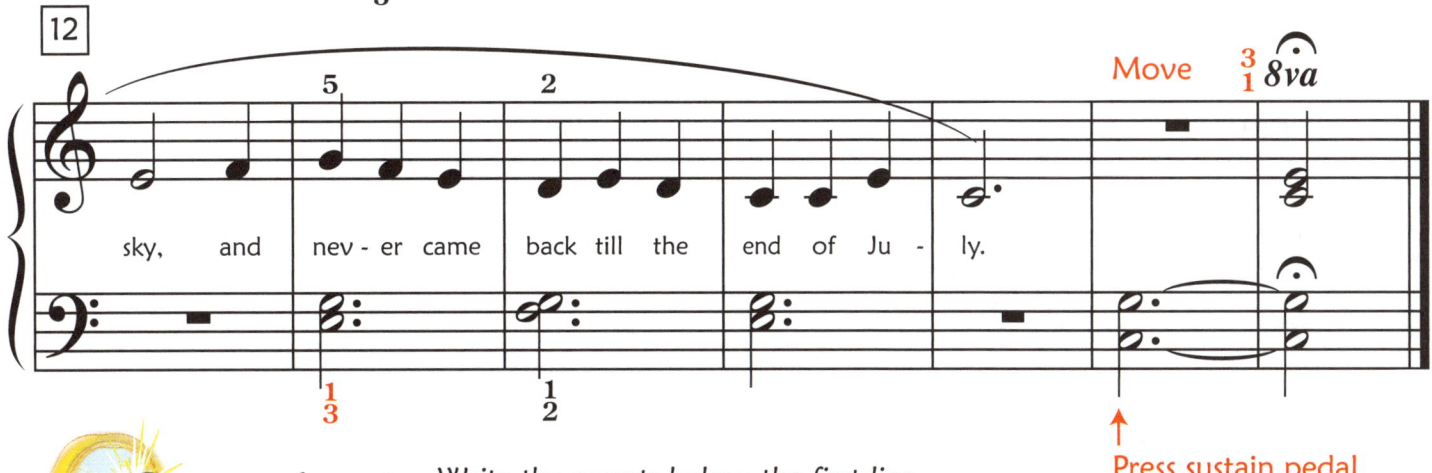

With humor

f I asked my moth-er for fif-ty pence, to see the el-e-phant jump the fence. He jumped so high that he touched the sky, and nev-er came back till the end of Ju-ly.

Move

LH over

LH over

Move

8va

Press sustain pedal and hold to end.

Closer Look — *Write the counts below the first line of music in* I Asked My Mother.

New Note D

A 2nd up from Middle C in bass clef.

New Rhythm

$\frac{4}{4}$ ♩ ♩ ♩ ♩ | ♩ ♩ ♩ :||

Count: 1 2 - 3 4   1 - 2 3 - 4

Tap and count aloud 3 times each day.

Broadway Star

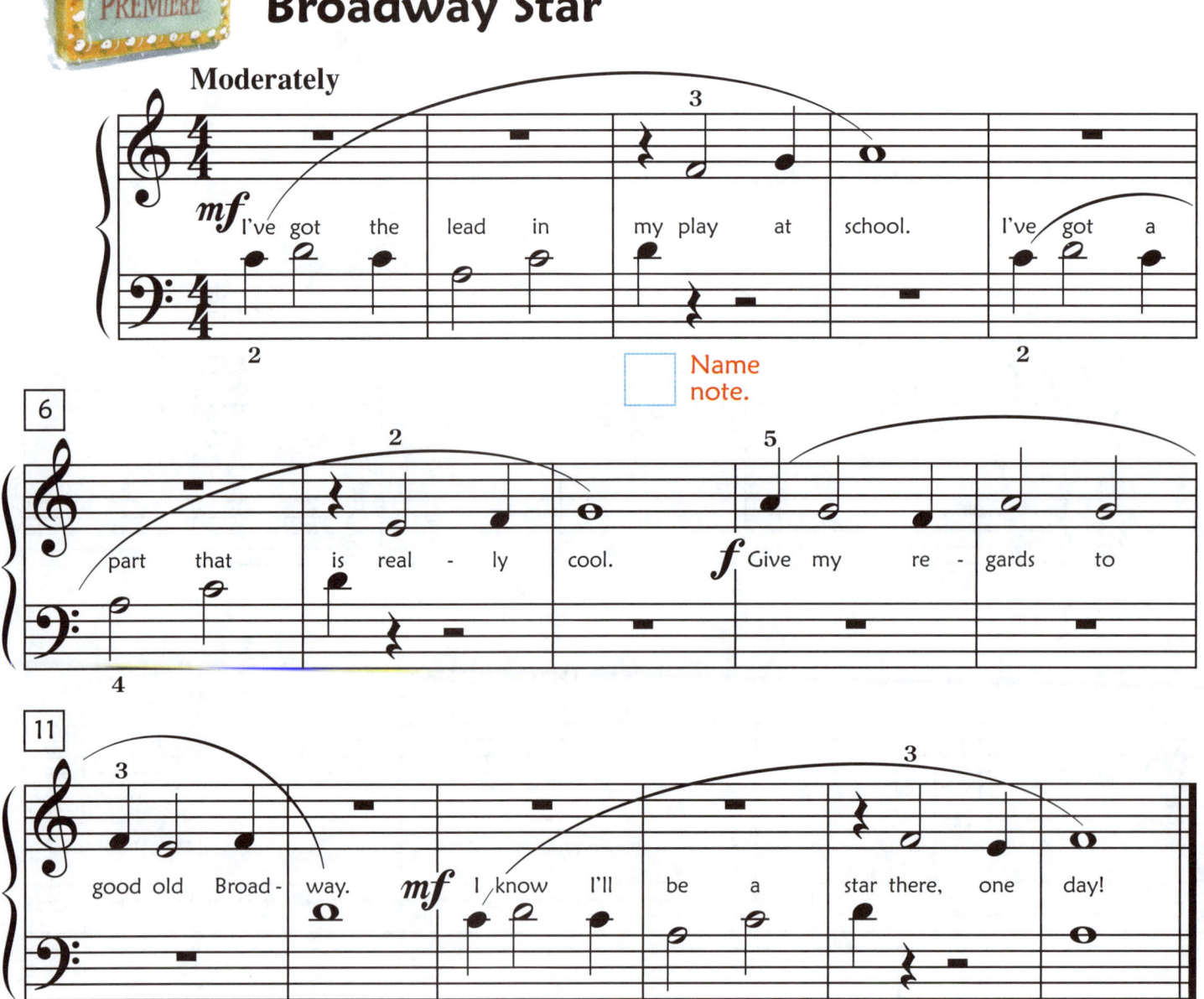

Moderately

I've got the lead in my play at school. I've got a part that is real-ly cool. *f* Give my re-gards to good old Broad-way. *mf* I know I'll be a star there, one day!

Duet: Student plays one octave higher.

The Joke

CD 61/62　GM 31

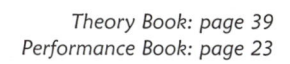

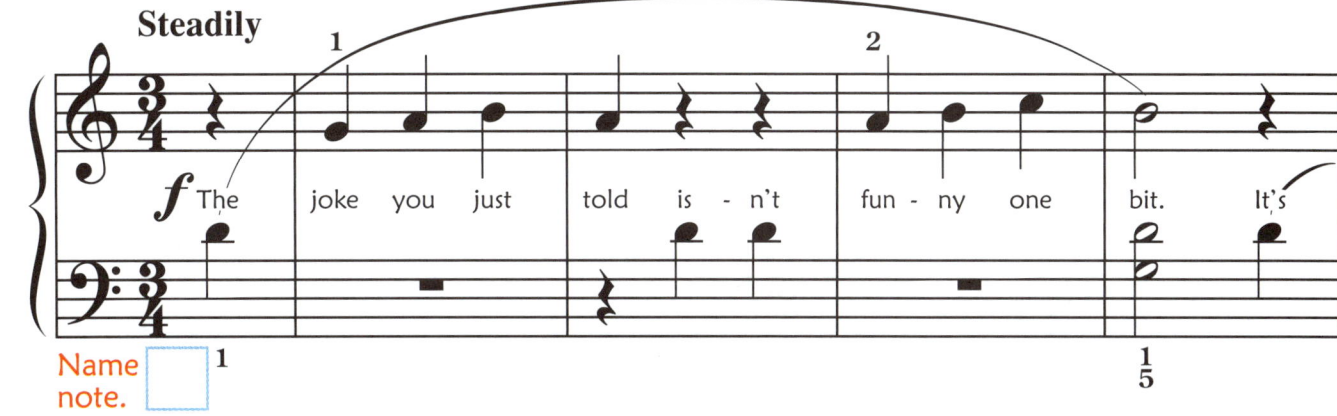

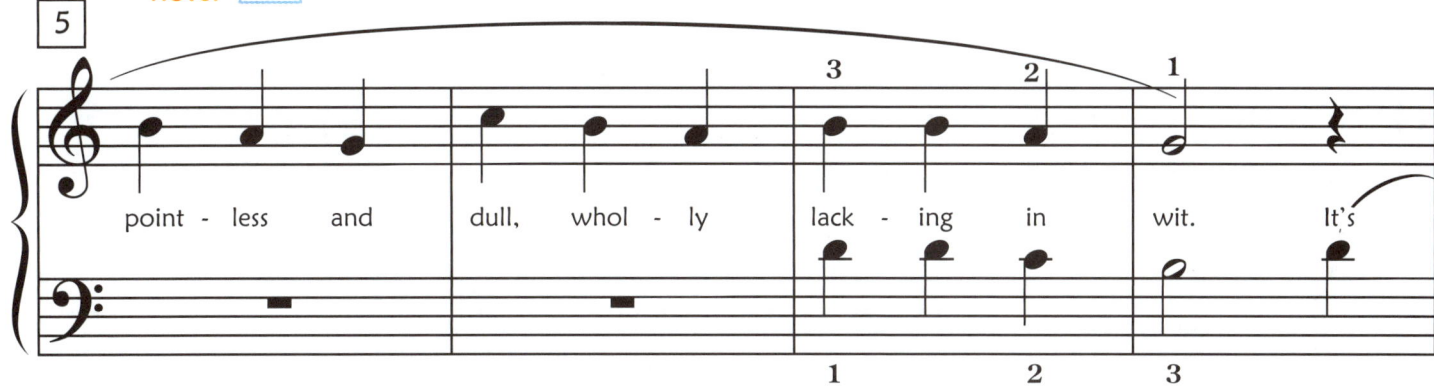

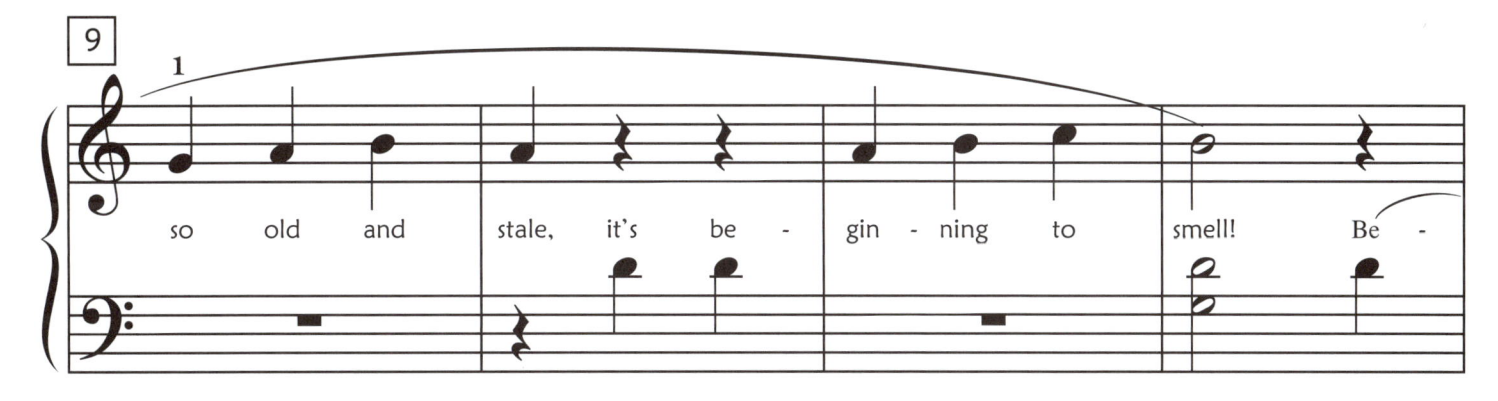

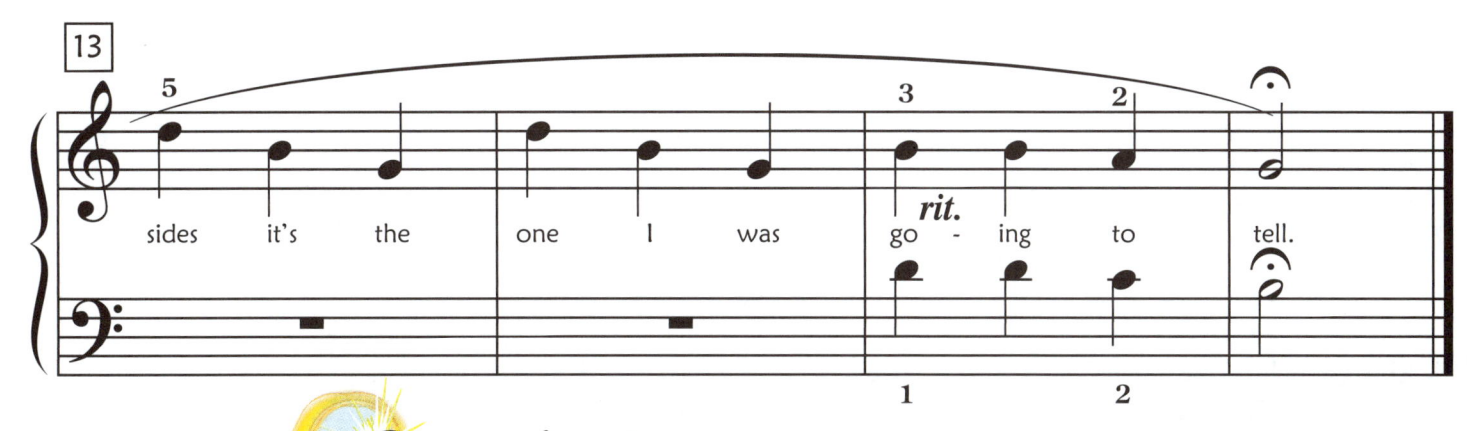

Workout 7 Hands Together

Steadily

The joke you just told is-n't fun-ny one bit. It's

Name note. ☐

point-less and dull, whol-ly lack-ing in wit. It's

so old and stale, it's be-gin-ning to smell! Be-

sides it's the one I was go-ing to tell.

rit.

Closer Look Write the counts below the first line of music in *The Joke*.

My Sombrero

CD 63/64   GM 32

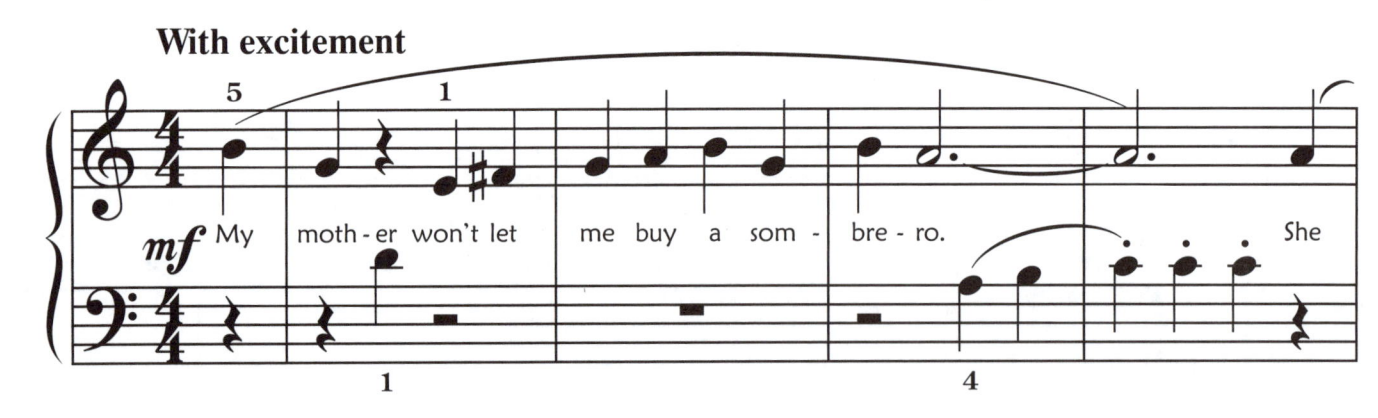

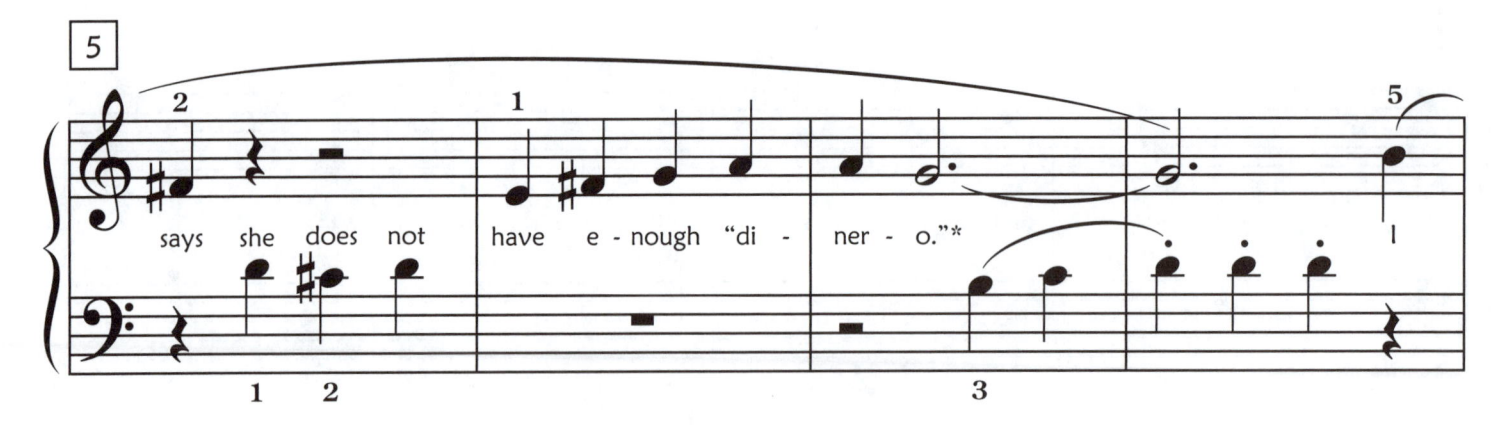

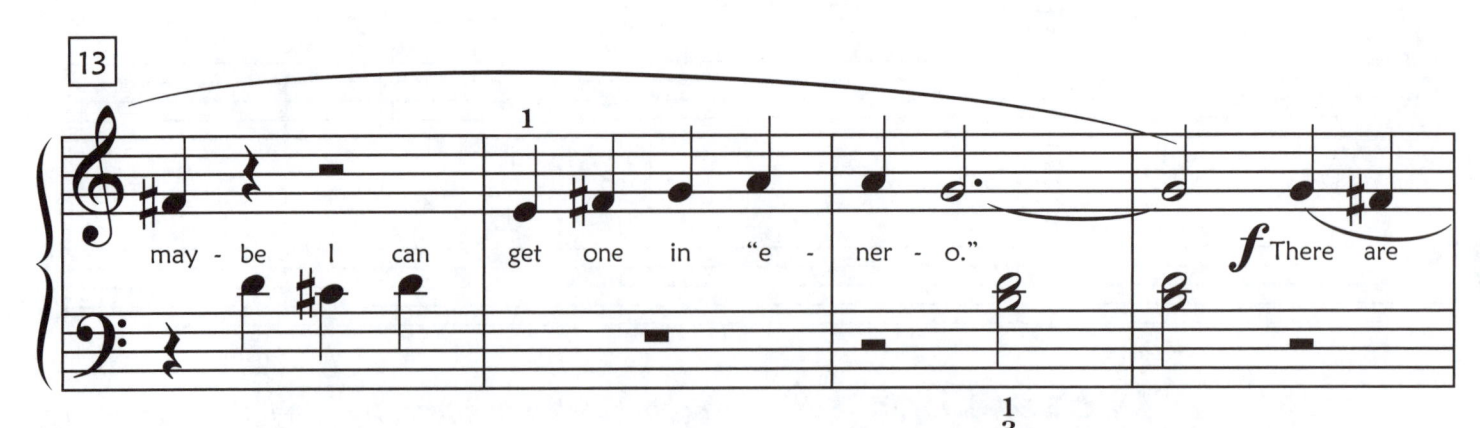

Workout 8 Hands Together

With excitement

My mother won't let me buy a sombrero. She says she does not have enough "dinero."* I guess I'll have to wait until "febrero," or maybe I can get one in "enero." There are

*dinero = money; febrero = February; enero = January

17
straw ones, there are felt ones, there are ones with fringe that sways. When I
21
put one on my head, I want to shout, "O - lé!" mf I'll
25
nev - er want to take off my som - bre - ro. I'll
29
want to wear it ev - 'ry - where that I go!

Moving Down a Semitone

Remember that the smallest interval on the keyboard is a **semitone.**

When moving *down* the keyboard, a semitone is the very next key to the *left*, black or white.

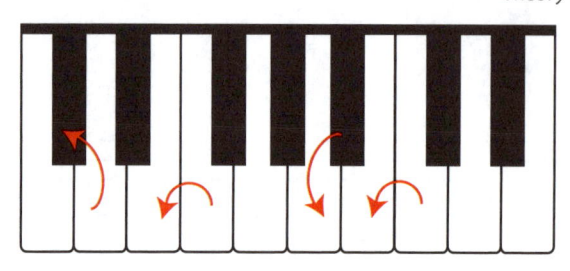

Circle one

- Play G, then the key a semitone lower. **black key** **white key**
- Play D, then the key a semitone lower. **black key** **white key**
- Play F, then the key a semitone lower. **black key** **white key**
- Play A, then the key a semitone lower. **black key** **white key**
- Play C, then the key a semitone lower. **black key** **white key**

Flat Sign

♭ A **flat** sign is the music symbol that *lowers* a note one semitone (to the left).

Sight-Reading

Play and say the note names as quickly as you can, 3 times each day. Use the correct fingering.

Write the name of each flat key marked with an X.   Note: F♭ and C♭ are white keys.

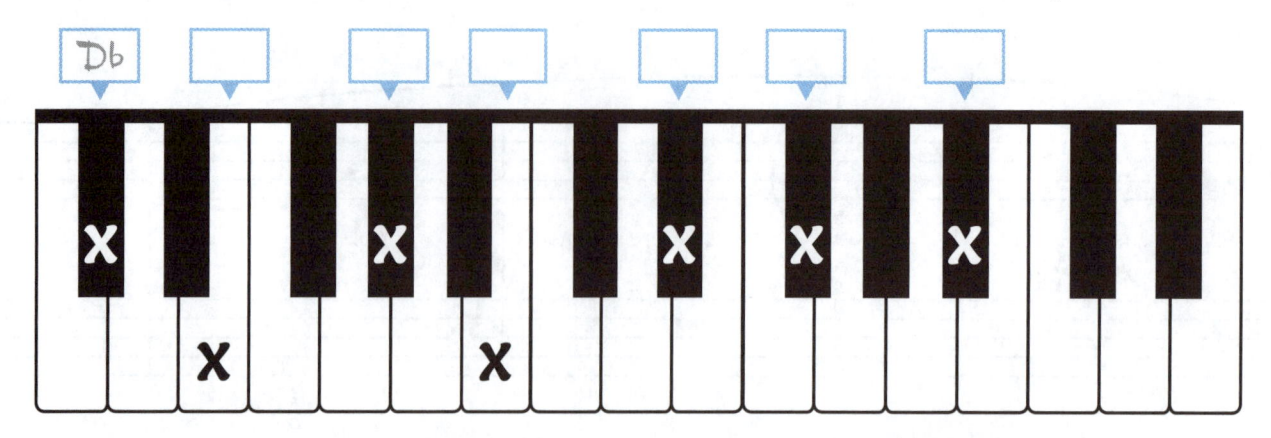

D♭

The Mythical Unicorn

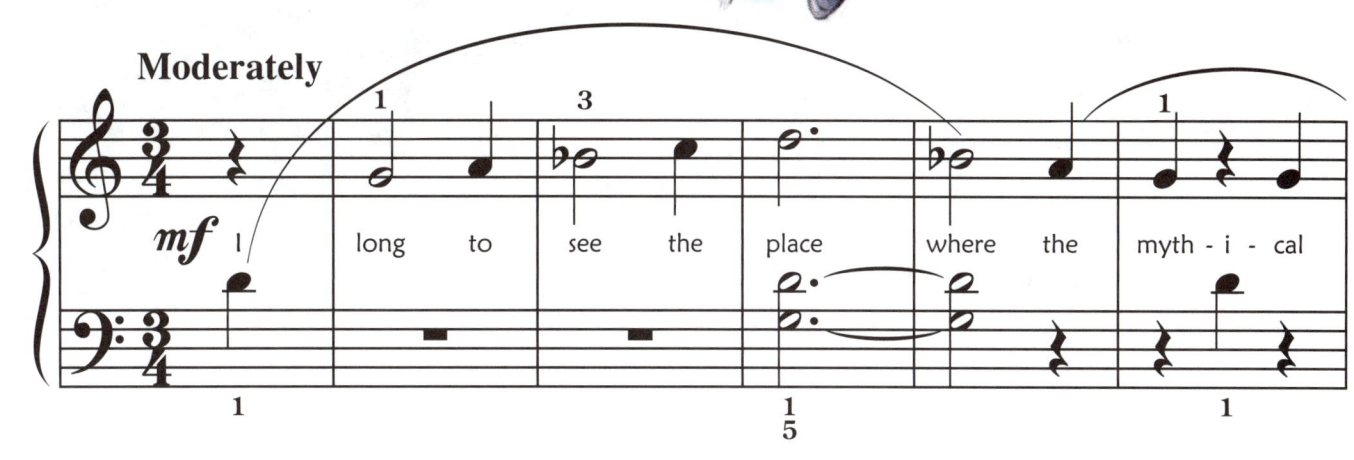

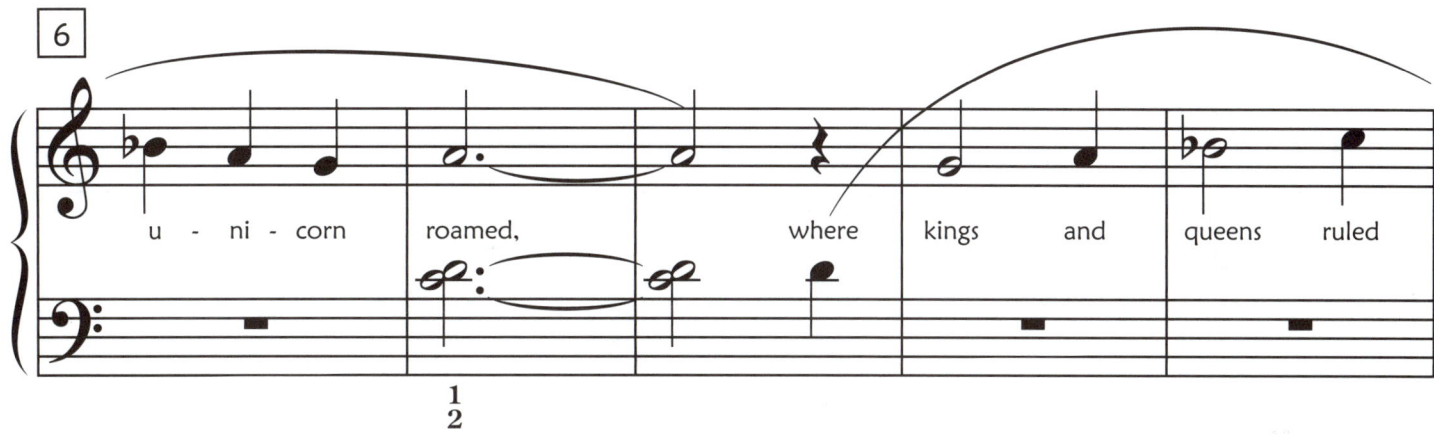

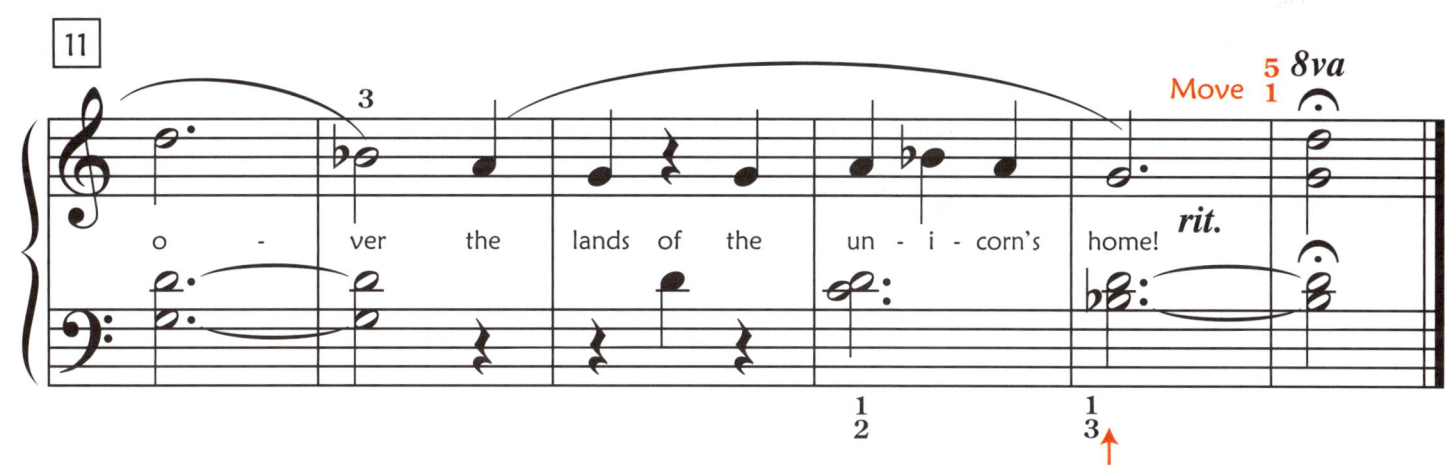

I long to see the place where the myth-i-cal u-ni-corn roamed, where kings and queens ruled o-ver the lands of the un-i-corn's home!

Press sustain pedal and hold to end when played without duet part.

Duet: Student plays one octave higher.

Like a sharp, a flat applies to the same note for the rest of the bar. The flat sign is cancelled by the bar line at the end of the bar.

Lunch Box Blues

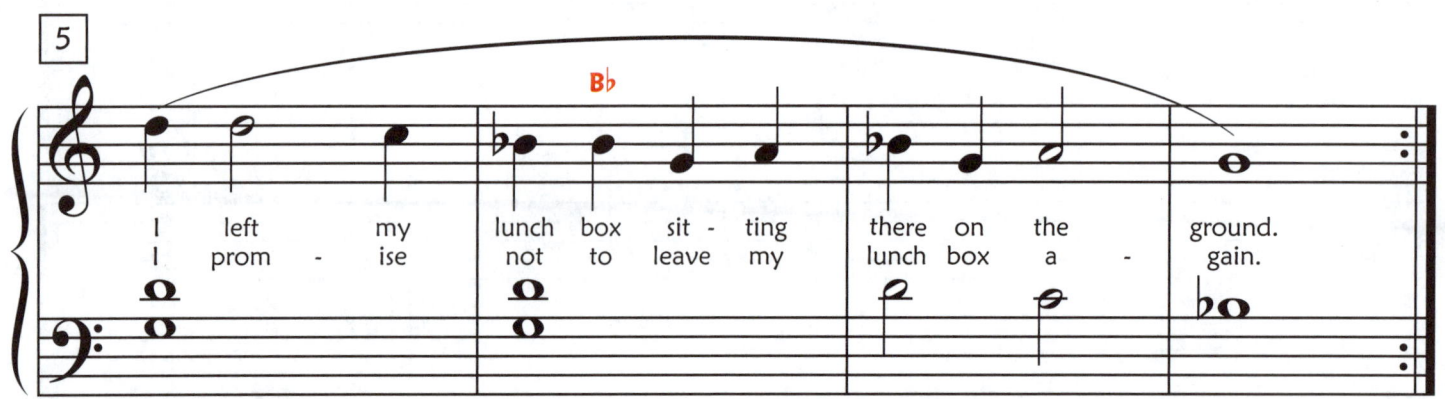

Slowly

Please, Mis - ter Bus Driv - er, turn a - round!
Thanks, Mis - ter Bus Driv - er, you're my friend!

I left my lunch box sit - ting there on the ground.
I prom - ise not to leave my lunch box a - gain.

Premier Performer

Play Lunch Box Blues *again without the duet, changing each B-flat to a B. Now play with B-flats on the first verse and B's on the second verse to change the mood.*

Duet: Student plays one octave higher.

Egyptian Pyramids

CD 69/70   GM 35

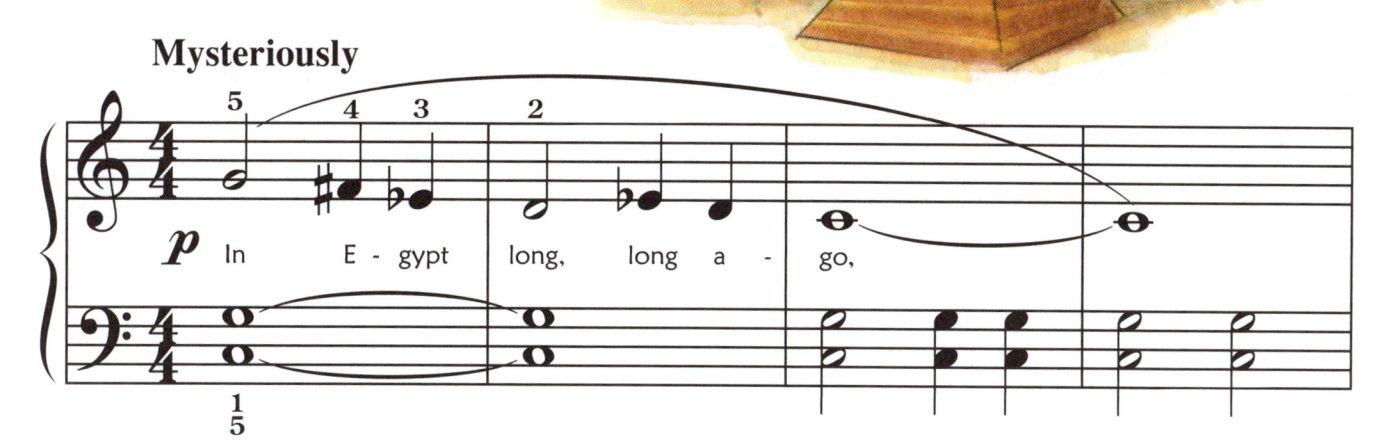

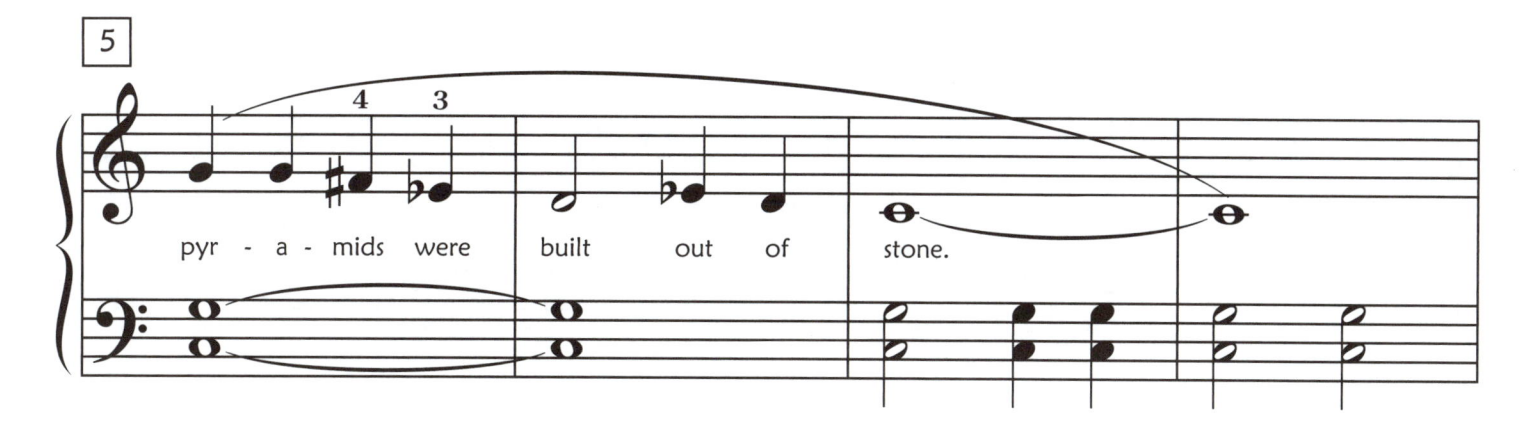

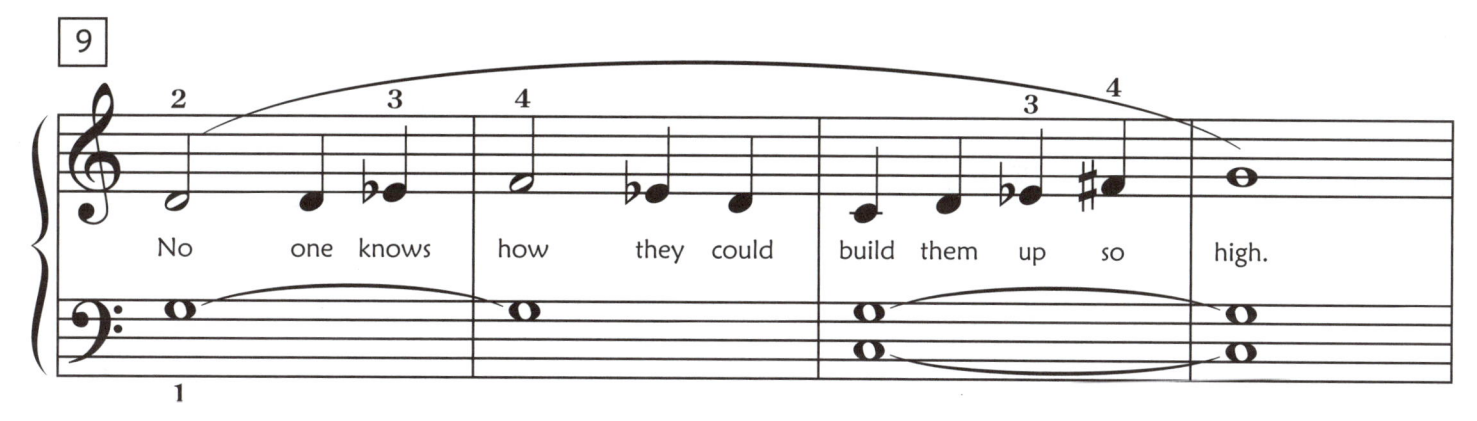

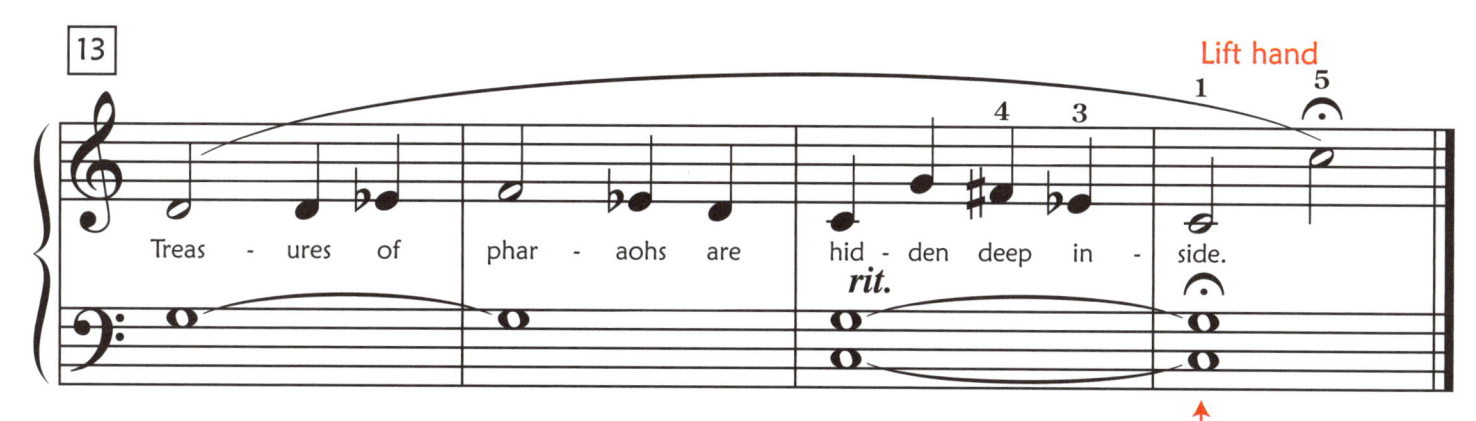

Theory Book: pages 45–46

Mysteriously

In E-gypt long, long a-go,

pyr-a-mids were built out of stone.

No one knows how they could build them up so high.

Treas-ures of phar-aohs are hid-den deep in-side.

rit.

Lift hand

Press sustain pedal and hold to end.

Premier Performer — Play *Egyptian Pyramids* again with RH one octave higher and LH one octave lower.

It's a Brand-New Day!

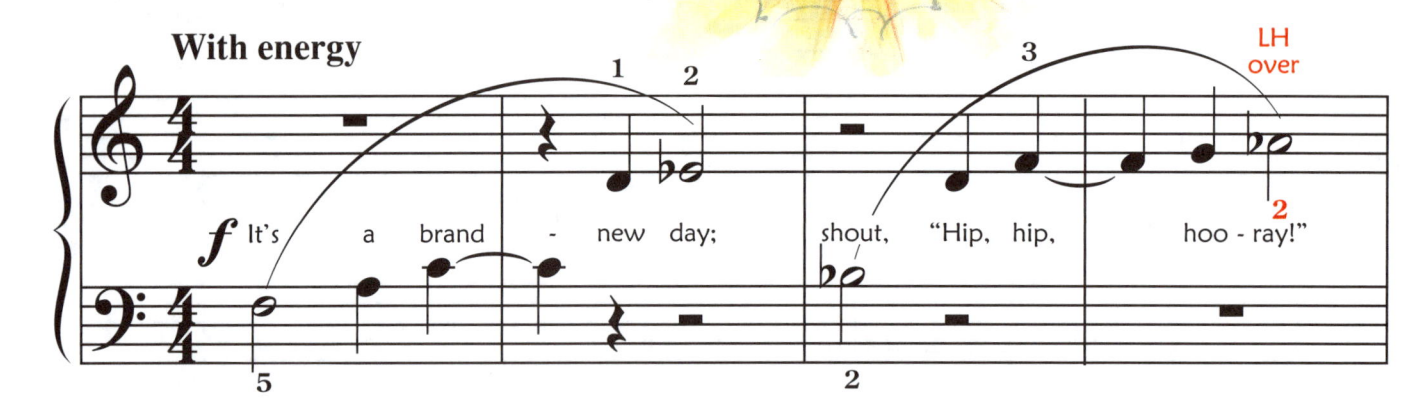

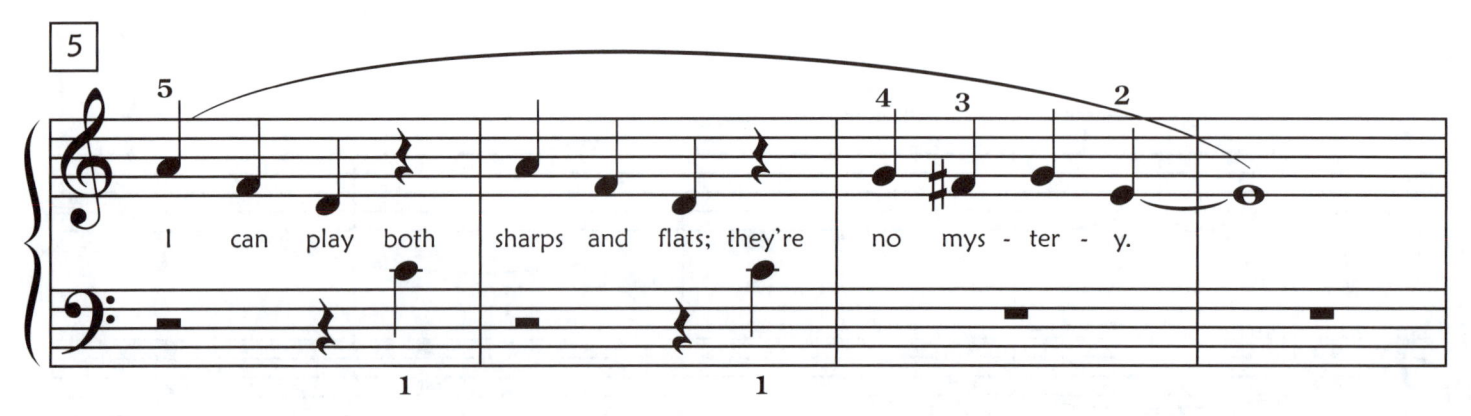

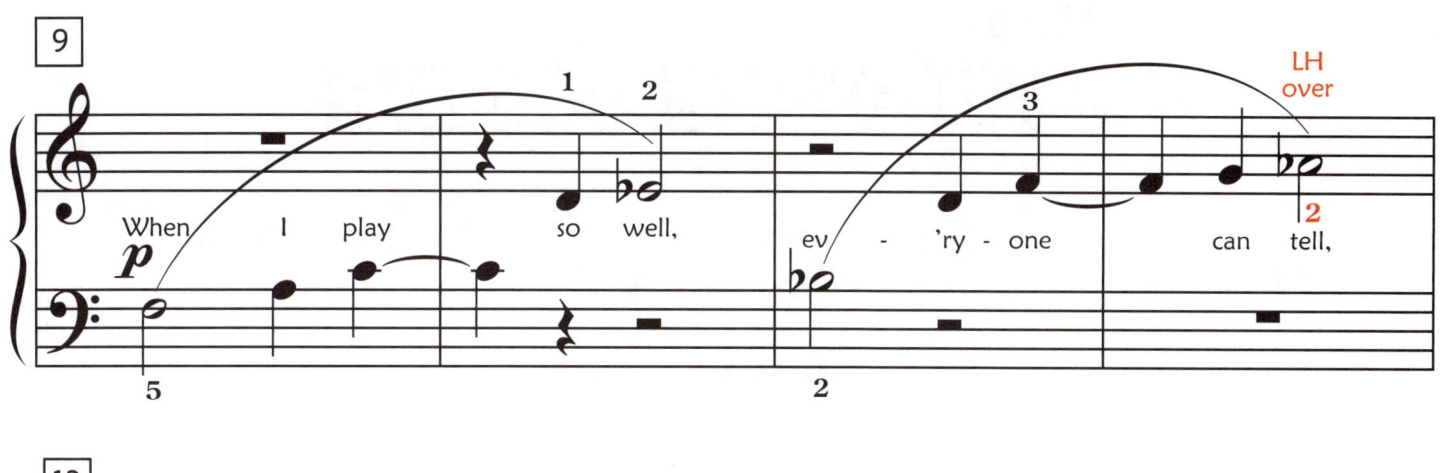

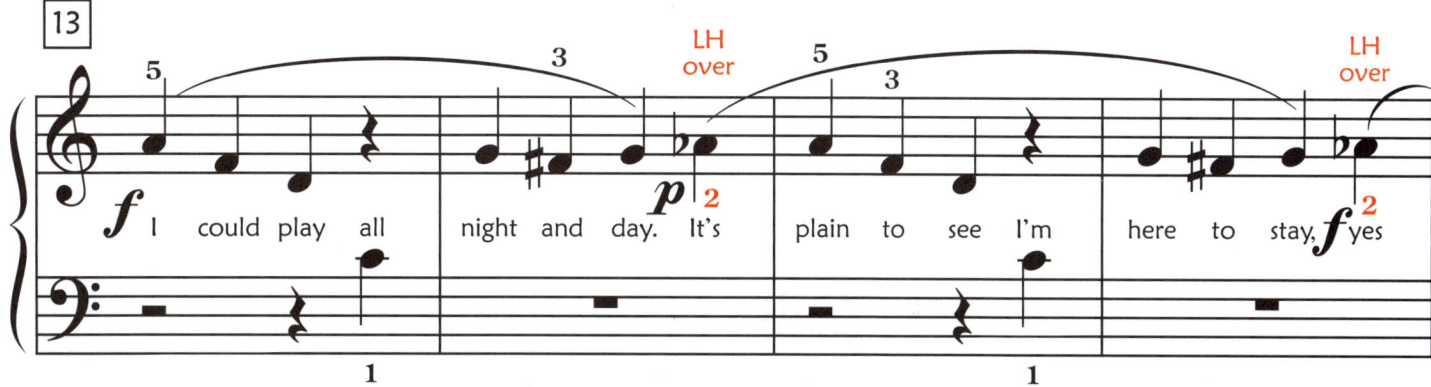

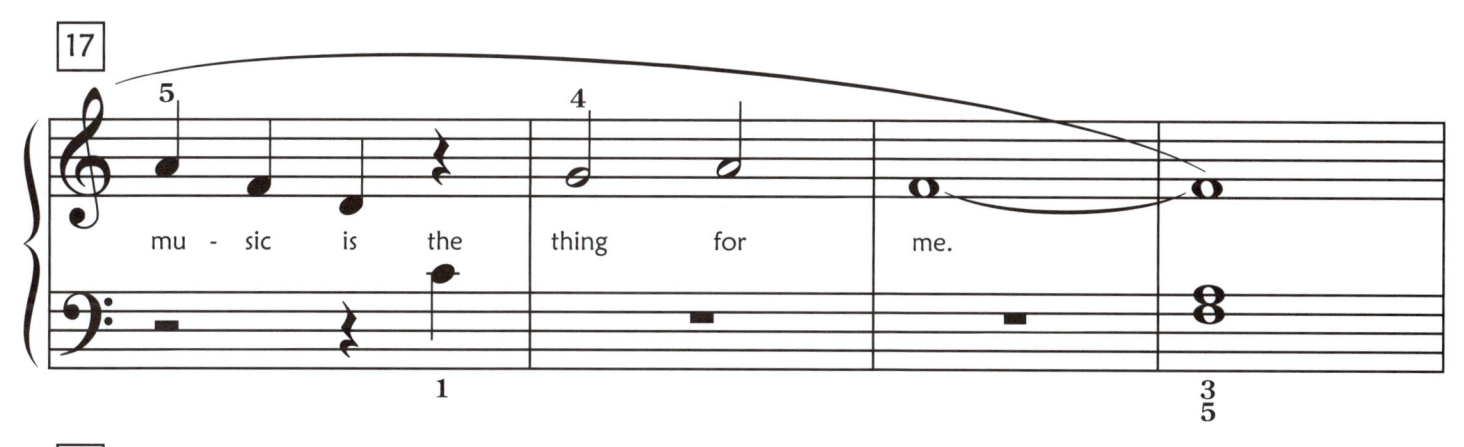

Closer Look — Find and name 3 different flats in *It's a Brand-New Day*. _____ _____ _____
Find and name 2 sharps. _____ _____

Alfred's Premier Performer Piano Achievement Award

presented to

_____
Student

You have
successfully completed
Lesson Book 1B
and are
hereby promoted to
Lesson Book 2A.

_____   _____
Teacher   *Date*